Fulfilling the Eye
ANTHONY ETEROVICH (1916 - 2011)

" The magic of Shakespeare with words, the thrill of Beethoven in music, is certainly a rewarding experience. But the human eye, being precious, demands another kind of fulfillment.

Color, design, their intertwining connotations have indescribable powers of their own - something quite personal to the artist and often to strongly related experiences of the observer."

Anthony Eterovich

Fulfilling the Eye

Published by: the Artists Archives of the Western Reserve
to accompany the exhibition of the same name

Designed by: Mindy Tousley
Contributing Editor: Megan Alves

Contributors include:
Thomas Roese
Karen Eterovich Maquire

Photography is courtesy of the Eterovich family, AAWR, and ARTneo

AAWR Support Staff:
Executive Director: Mindy Tousley
Gallery and Archives Coordinator: Megan Alves
Registrar: Kelly Pontoni

AAWR Board of Directors:
Stuart Pearl, President
Cris Drugan, Vice President
David Joranko, Treasurer
Lee Heinen, Secretary

Philip Bautista
Michael Bowen
Stephen Bucchieri
Ryn Clarke
Suzan Kraus
Dr. Vincent Monnier
Jocelyn Ruf
Rota Sackerlotzky
John Sargent III

Copyright 2019 The Artists Archives of the Western Reserve
All Rights Reserved

Fulfilling the Eye

ANTHONY ETEROVICH (1916 - 2011)
November 21, 2019 - January 20, 2020

Presented by
The Artists Archives of the Western Reserve
1834 E 123rd St., Cleveland, Ohio 44106

Cover image: *Green Curly Haired Boy,* mixed media on paper, 36" x 24"

Introduction and Acknowledgement

Anthony Eterovich is the seventy first artist to be accepted into the Archives. His work was given to the collection through the generosity of his widow, Alice Eterovich, and his daughter Karen Eterovich Maguire.

The title for this solo exhibition, "Fulfilling the Eye", was taken from the following typewritten quote attributed to Anthony by his daughter.

"The magic of Shakespeare with words, the thrill of Beethoven in music, is certainly a rewarding experience. But the human eye, being precious, demands another kind of fulfillment. Color, design, their intertwining connotations have indescribable powers of their own - something quite personal to the artist and often to strongly related experiences of the observer."

This quote certainly describes the philosophy behind the fluid, exuberant lines of Eterovich's drawings, as well as the vibrant color combinations of his expressive watercolors and the magical realist paintings completed later in his life. Eterovich was an impressive draughtsman, completing beautiful portraits of his contemporaries in his teen age years, well before the time he spent at the Art Students League, where such drawing skills were prized. He in turn demanded much of in terms of the drawing skills of his own students when he later took up the role of teacher. It was important to me when selecting the work for this exhibition to include a number of these early drawings, as well as examples of his later painting styles. Subsequently the work in *fulfilling the Eye* covers five decades including more than thirty pieces borrowed from the Archives collection, ARTneo and the Eterovich estate. Of particular note are Eterovich's gestural watercolor portraits whose color combinations and delicacy of line harken back to the influences of The Cleveland School.

While I did not have the pleasure of knowing Anthony Eterovich while he was alive, his teaching and exhibition records speak volumes about the energy and charisma of the man, and the value of his work as an artist. The Archives is very proud to hold this inaugural exhibition in his honor, and to welcome a sample of his work into our permanent collection.

I would like to acknowledge and thank all of those who support the Artists Archives of the Western Reserve, and make exhibitions like this one possible. Thank you to Megan Alves, Gallery and Archives Coordinator, Kelly Pontoni our Registrar, William Tregoning, the AAWR Exhibition Committee chaired by John Sargent III, as well as all the other members and volunteers including our dedicated Board of Directors. A very special thank you to the David E Davis Art Foundation which has continued to support the dream of our founder, David Davis, for the past twenty seven years. Last, but not least, thank you to Alice Eterovich, Karen Eterovich Maguire, and Anthony Eterovich. The contributions of all of our eighty four Archived Artists comprise an important slice of Ohio history and placing their work in the Archives ensures that these legacies will not be lost to future generations.

Mindy Tousley
AAWR Executive Director 2019

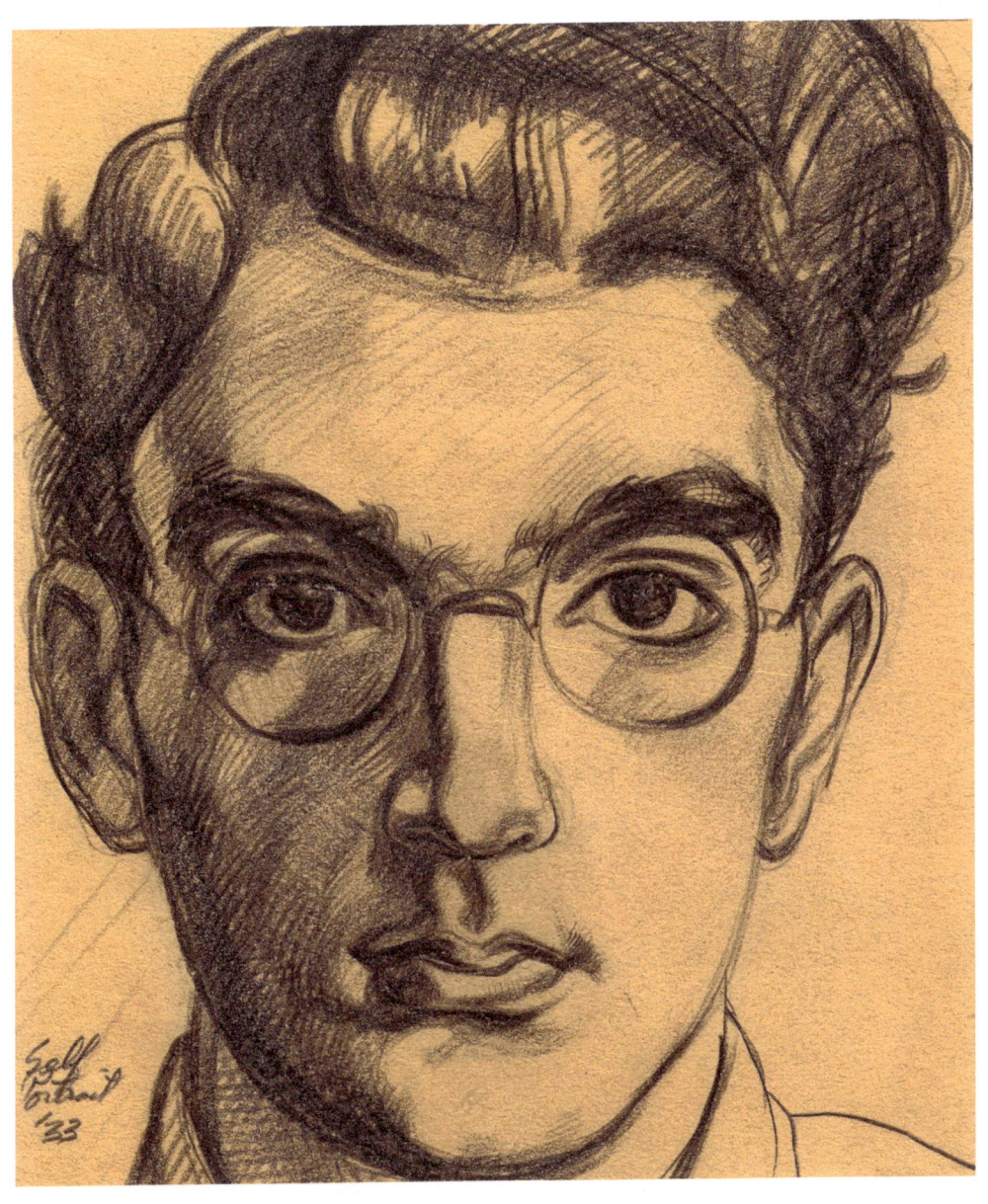

Self Portrait charcoal on paper   9 x 7.5" 1933
collection of the Eterovich family

Anthony Eterovich (1916 - 2011)

"Painting is the thrilling act which ... encompasses a battleground of contradictions all to be resolved without compromise." Anthony W. Eterovich 1916-2011

Anthony William Eterovich was born in Cleveland, Ohio on April 2, 1916, the youngest of three surviving children. His parents, George and Anna, had emigrated from the Dalmatian coast of what is now Croatia to Cleveland. The family settled on the west side along with other Eastern European immigrants, and George worked in the steel mills. Somehow recognizing the essence of a gift in his son, George Eterovich saw to it that, from the time he was three, Anthony had a pencil in his hand and that he was provided with the materials he needed to express himself on paper. George had a stroke and died while Anthony was still a teenager, and consequently all three children were sent to work. Anthony began packing potatoes for a grocer while still attending school, and continued his role as an artist by working as the cartoonist for the school paper. In the early 1930's he met and studied with John Teyral at the Merrick House Settlement which provided community services in Tremont for immigrant families.

In 1934, Eterovich won a scholarship to the Cleveland Institute of Art where he received a degree in portraiture in 1938. In addition, he began exhibiting in the Cleveland Museum of Art May Shows in 1934 at the very young age of 18. Over the course of his lengthy career Mr. Eterovich had a total of 55 works exhibited at May Shows from 1934 to 1971. To earn money while in art school Eterovich started teaching at the Merrick House Settlement in 1936. He was encouraged as an artist and teacher by Viktor Schreckengost who occasionally turned classes over to Anthony for a few hours each week.

During World War II, Eterovich was drafted. While in the US Army he achieved the rank of Sergeant Tech Four and completed more than thirty portraits of his peers, colonels, captains and a three star general. He was called upon to draw maps and create topographical visualizations of landing and occupied areas and silhouette identification of enemy aircraft and other vehicles. In addition, he taught French while stationed in Indian Town Gap, Pennsylvania from 1943-1944 and then Camp Gordon Johnston in Florida from 1944-1945.

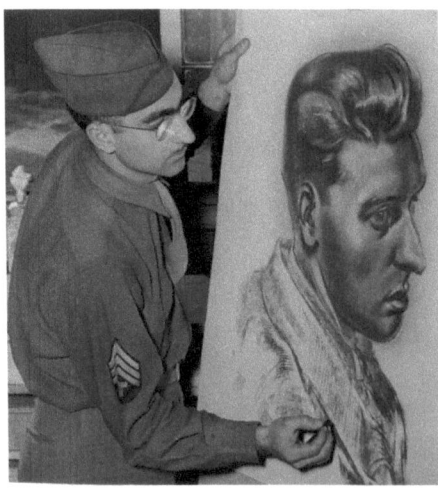

Photograph of Anthony Eterovich in the army.

After the army, Anthony went on to receive a Bachelor of Science in Education and a Masters Degree in Art Education from Western Reserve University in 1947. In 1947, he also won a First Prize Purchase Award from the Cleveland Museum of Art in the Etching category for "Suzanne", as part of the May show that year. He continued his education with honors in extended studies at Ohio University from 1948-1949. In 1950, he married Alice Troyan, who had recently graduated from Kent State University with a major in Physical Education. The pair spent their summers in New York City and Anthony attended the New York Art Students League from 1950-1954. While Eterovich studied at the League, he took his work to a who's who of art dealers, including Edith Halpert and Harry Salpeter while Alice studied modern dance with Martha Graham and Eric Hawkins.

Eterovich achieved nationwide recognition when he won another First Prize Purchase award in the 1951 Sixteenth Annual New Year's Show, a national art competition at the Butler Institute for American Art with an abstract oil painting entitled "The Merry Bench". Edith Halpert juried this competition, and asked Eterovich for another painting to hang in her New York City Gallery. This painting was reviewed by Howard Devree in the New York Times on May 6, 1951, who said,

> "One of the most ambitious canvases is by Anthony Eterovich of Cleveland – 'Table Charade', which might have been called 'The World is full of a Number of Things' and succeeds in bringing organization out of what might well have been a too complicated profusion of detail."

During his lifetime Anthony Eterovich participated in more than one hundred and fifty exhibitions, including the Cleveland Museum of Art May Shows; the Circle Gallery, the Butler Institute of American Art, the Junior Chamber of Commerce Jay Shows, the Canton Art Institute, the Massillon Museum of Art, the Ohio State Fair, Ohio University, Cleveland Public Schools Art Teachers Shows, the Chautauqua Institute, Musicarnival, West Shorer Concerts in Lakewood, a Festival of Arts Champagne Dinner featuring Dame Judith Anderson, the Annual Park Synagogue Art Festival, the Jewish Community Center and Cleveland Institute of Art Faculty Shows from 1950 to 2003.

Until his death in 2011, Eterovich's work was only seen collectively in two solo shows. He had twenty oil paintings on view at the Women's City Club in 1956 and a charcoal drawing show at the Intown Club in 1963. Both shows were favorably reviewed by Marie Kirkwood of the Cleveland Plain Dealer. Other exhibits in the area included the Greenbrier Cultural Center in Parma Heights and the Country Inn and Stables at Walden in Aurora, Ohio.

Eterovich's paintings incorporate abstract portraiture or photo realistic cityscapes. His work is known for color and imaginative, almost whimsical choices of subject matter. Eterovich was impacted by his immigrant Croatian family, living through the Great Depression and serving in the Army during World War II. Artistic influences include Cleveland School artists, John Teyral, Carl Gaertner, Edmund Brucker, Viktor Schreckengost, Daniel Bosa, Ted Gorka and Peter Paul Dubaniewicz to name a few. He admired Renoir, Degas and Manet for color and Edward Hopper and Richard Estes for cityscapes and photo realism. He met and was judged by Edward Hopper when Hopper juried the exhibition for the Butler Institute of American Art in 1953. He studied with Jack Levine and Alexander Yakovleff; both had guest residencies at the Cleveland Institute of Art and left profound impressions on him. Artist/teachers who influenced his work also include Aaron Bohrod at Ohio University and Robert Motherwell at Oberlin College. In the mid-fifties he met and interviewed the Croatian artist and sculptor Ivan Mestrovic.

Mr. Eterovich taught for more than forty years for the Cleveland Public School System starting at Kennard Middle School. He moved to Rawlings Middle School, then Lincoln High School, and then he chaired the art department of Rhodes High School from 1962 to 1978. In 1974, he obtained a major grant from the Union of Independent Colleges of Art to develop a drawing program for EMR students. He was chairman of the Regional Scholastic Art Competition from 1981 to 1989. In 2014 a classroom was named for him in the new Cleveland Institute of Art Joseph McCullough Building. He is now part of the permanent collections of the Butler Institute of American Art, the Cleveland Museum of Art, The Artists Archives of the Western Reserve, ARTneo and the Southern Ohio Museum.

This biography is courtesy of Karen Eterovich Maquire, 2019

There are times in one's life when the unique happens. To know Anthony Eterovich, would be one of those unique happenings. Eterovich was rarely subtle, always dramatic, and full of non-stop energy. This artist, this teacher was a man in motion. A conversation with Anthony Eterovich would be a conversation animated with excessive and enthusiastic gesturing, dramatic pauses, or startling pronouncements, punctuated with props which might include clippings of articles, photos, books, or other supportive materials.

Eterovich started his formal career with a full scholarship to the Cleveland Institute of Art (CIA) in the late 1930's. In addition to the CIA, his educational credentials included the Western Reserve University (MA), Ohio University, and four years at the New York Art Students League.

In the classroom, Eterovich was usually on fire. Demonstrations of drawing and painting techniques were a regular occurrence. He omitted little, in terms of teaching technical applications and skills, but imagination and creativity were required from the student. Thought, critical thinking, **and** mastering of drawing skills was expected, if not demanded. Students entering his classroom at the Cleveland Public Schools, James Ford Rhodes High School, would be visually bombarded. Student work was pinned to every wall surface. Often this arrangement changed on a **daily** basis. Work was arranged in ascending order of success, with the ultimate prize being work positioned on the back wall...the "A" wall!

A list of his exhibitions is impressive. This list is particularly noteworthy when one considers the exhibition schedule ran simultaneously with a full public school teaching load, and as an adult education instructor at the Cleveland Institute of Art. On the list would be fifty-two years of faculty exhibitions at the Cleveland Institute of Art; thirty-seven years of May Shows at the Cleveland Museum of Art; thirty-three years of exhibiting at the Butler Institute of America Art; in addition to other exhibitions at various galleries, universities, and institutions throughout his long career.

A rich legacy is left in Anthony Eterovich's wake. An impressive collection of quality art distributed in many museums, corporate collections, and archives. There are countless artists, who were former students, who were inspired, taught, encouraged, and prepared to be practicing, professional artists who matriculated from his classroom. Once one was exposed to his pedagogy, or his art work, one was transformed.

Thomas Roese 2019

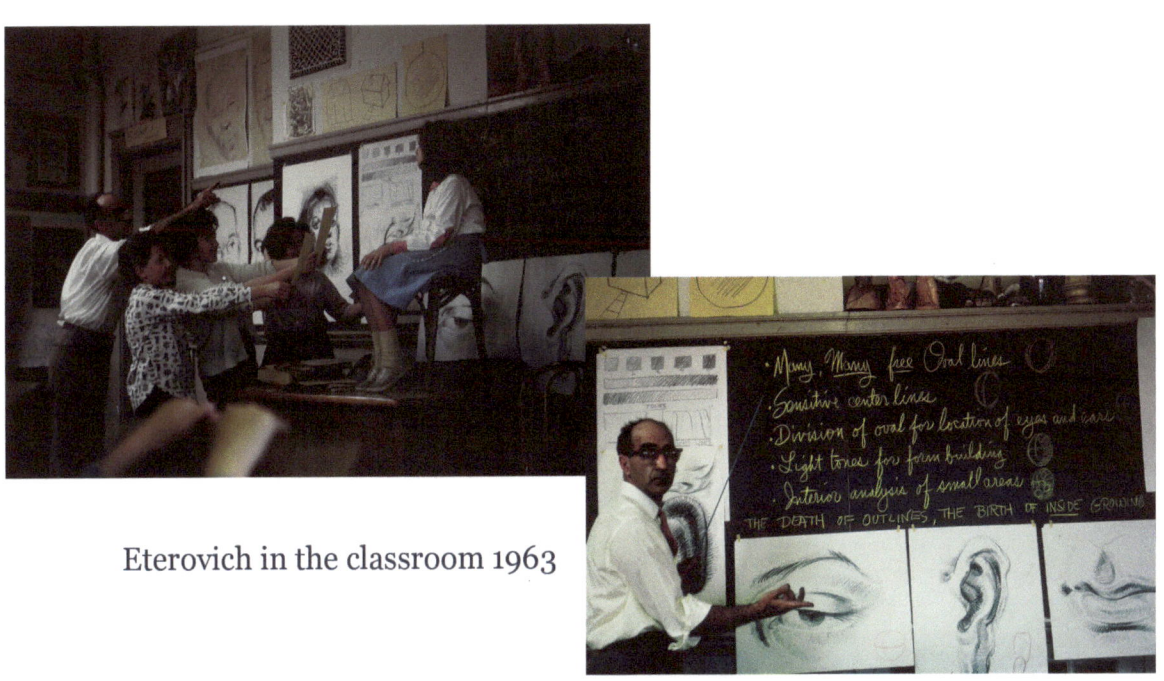

Eterovich in the classroom 1963

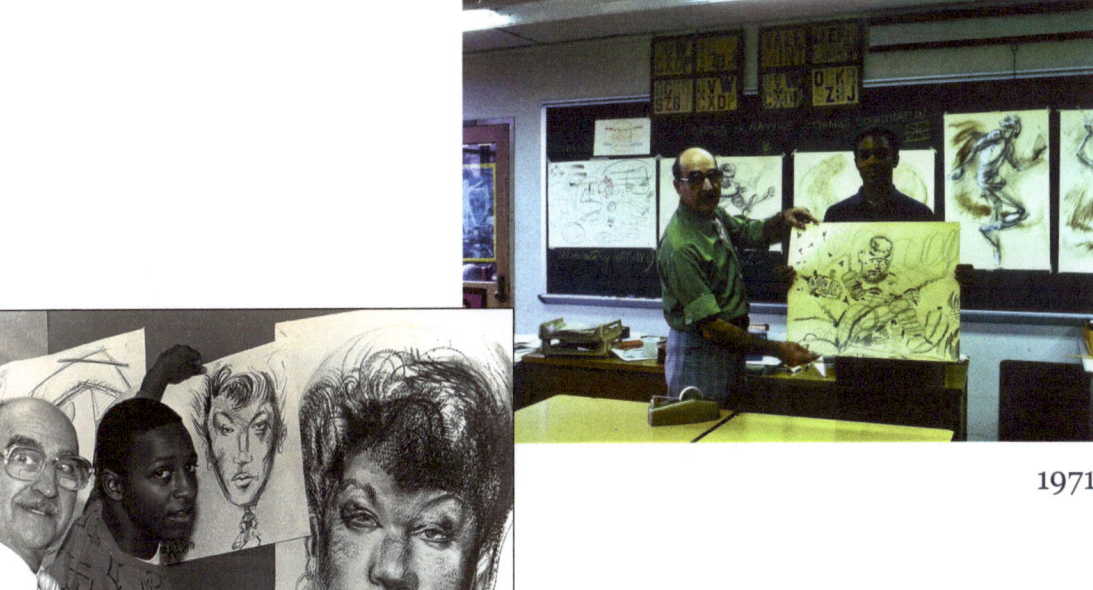

1971

1980

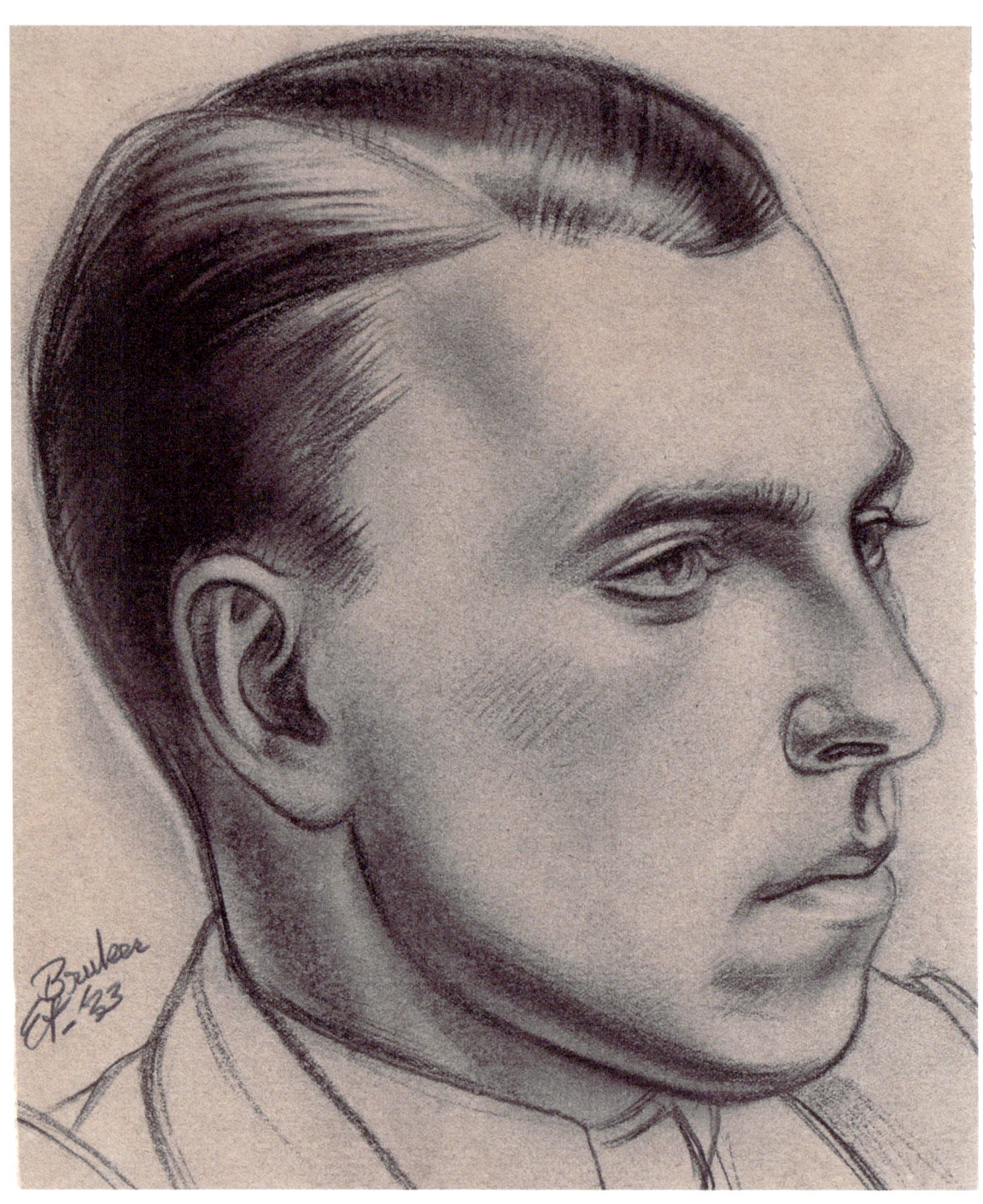

Portrait of Brucker   ebony pencil on paper   8.5 x 7.5"   1933
collection of the Eterovich family

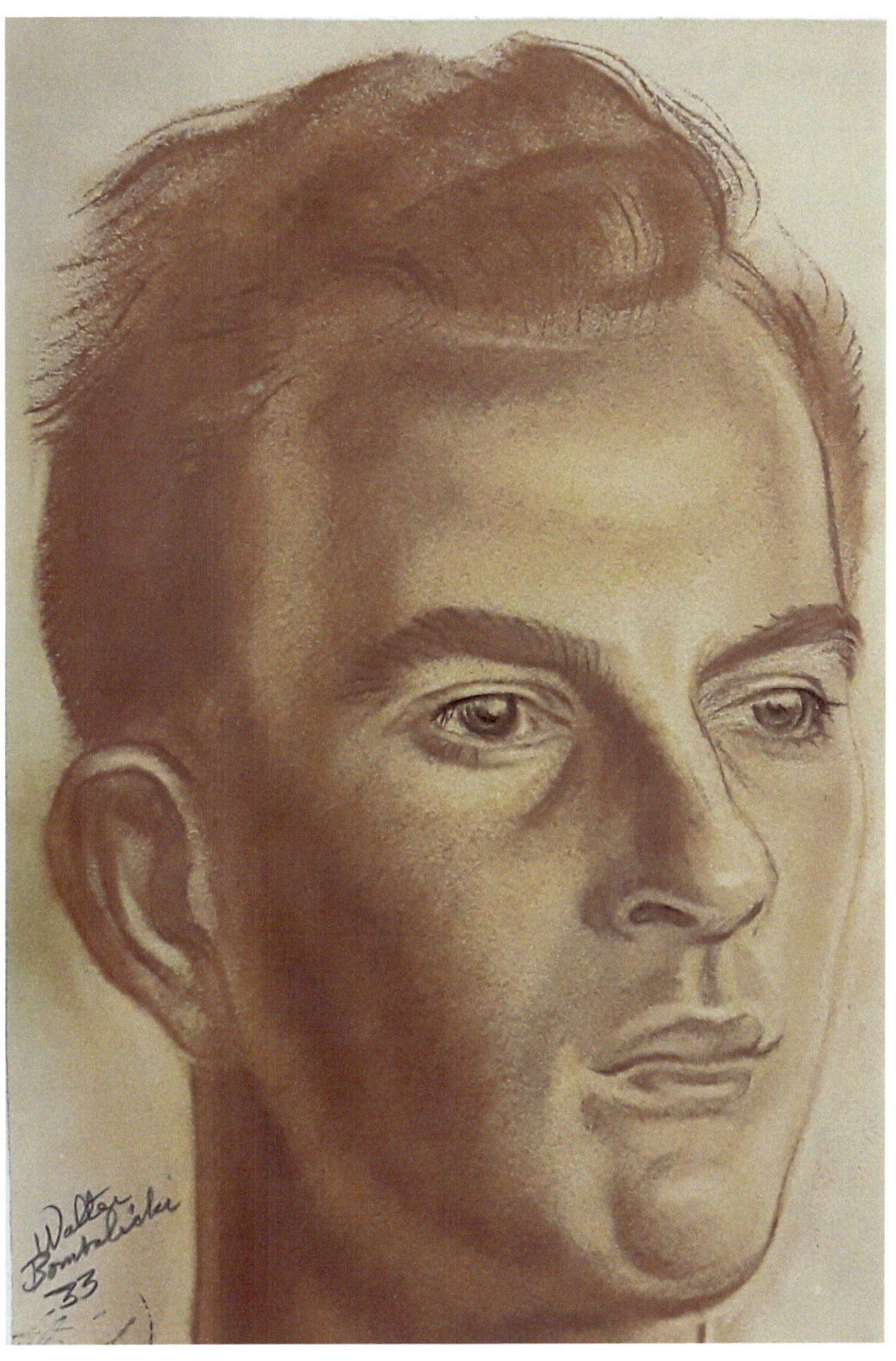

Walter Bombalicki charcoal on paper 10 x 7" 1933
collection of the Eterovich family

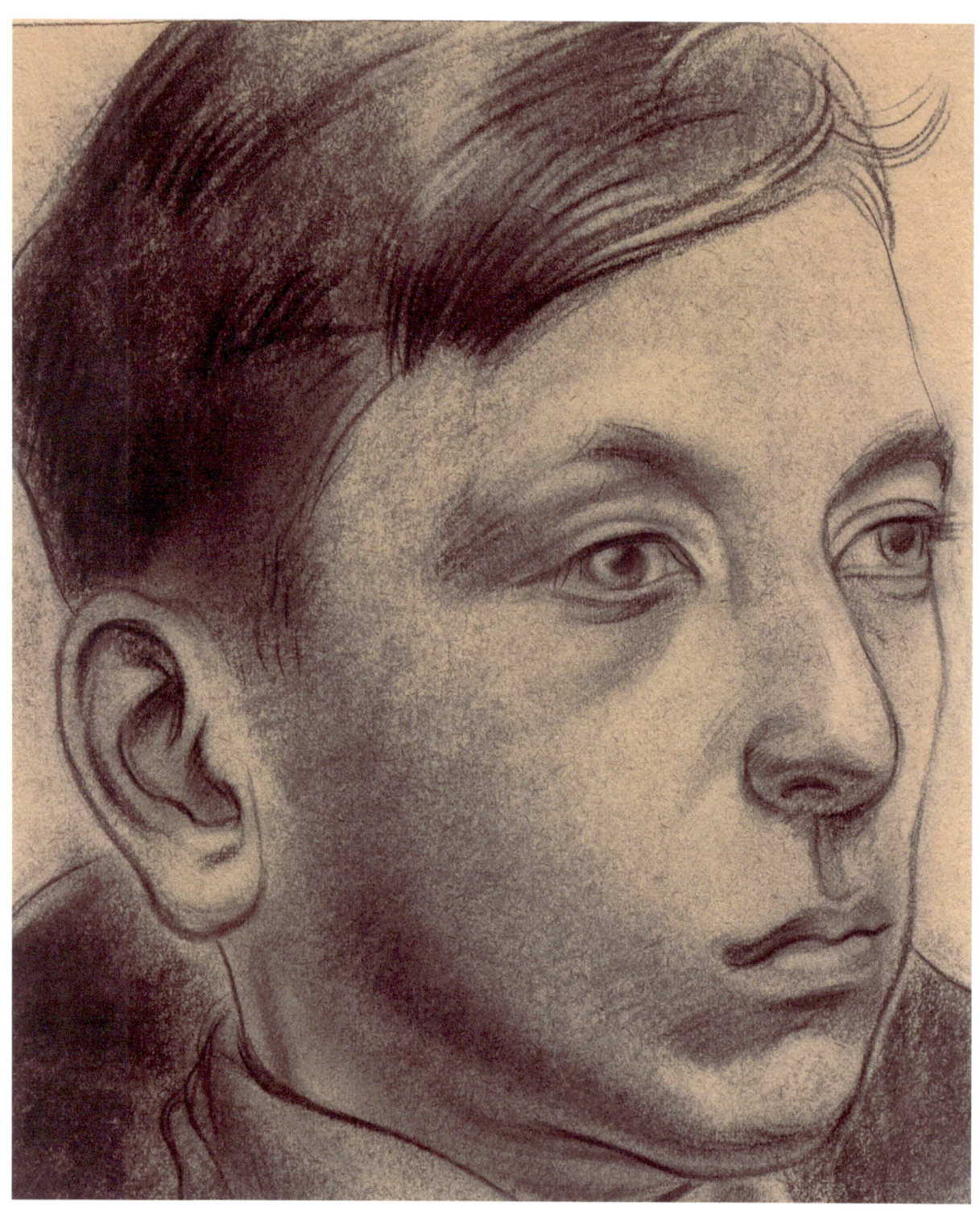

Untitled (Depression Boy) ebony pencil on paper 8.5 x 7.5" 1932
collection of the Eterovich family

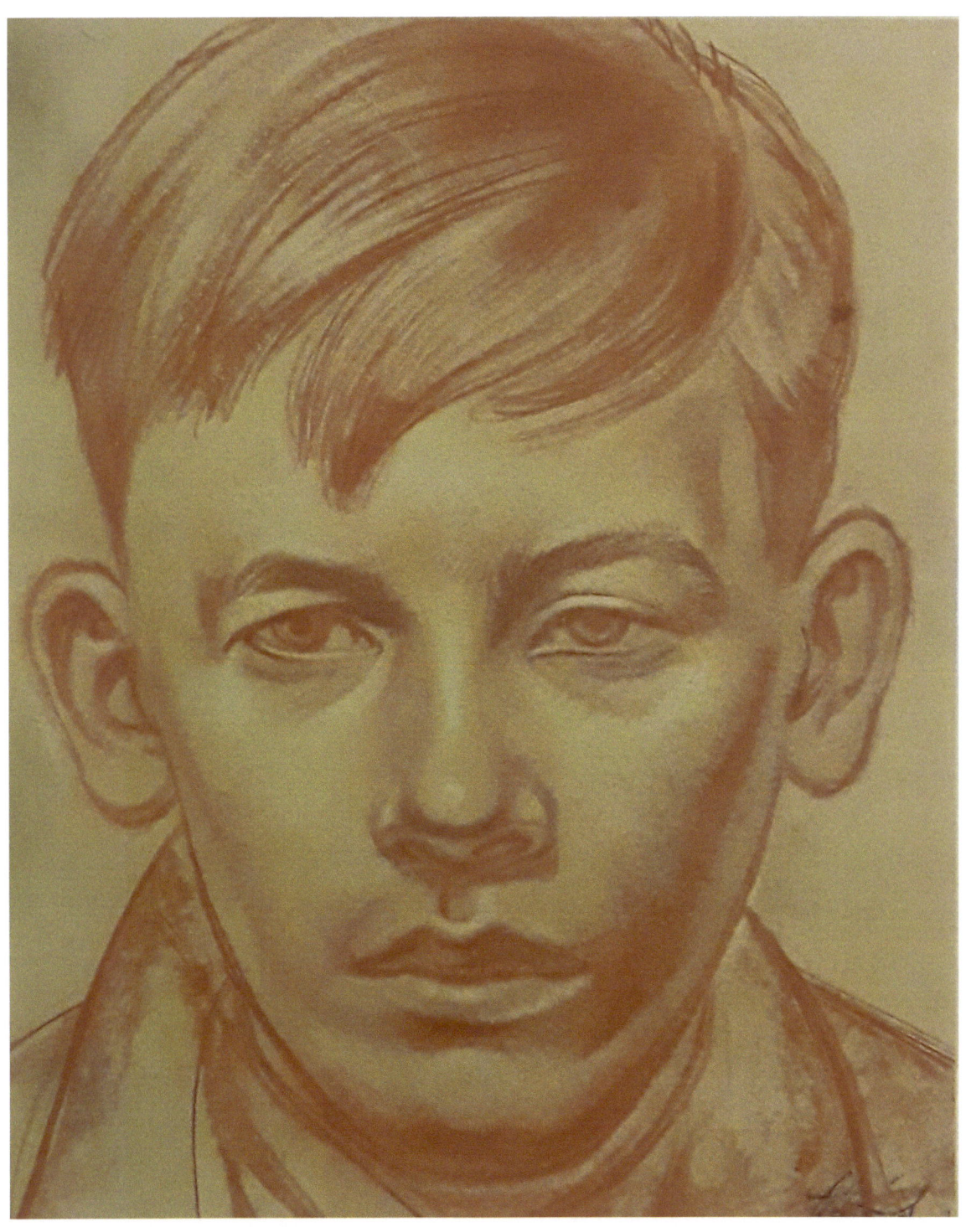

Untitled (Depression Boy)   charcoal on paper   8.5 x 7.5"   1932
collection of the Eterovich family

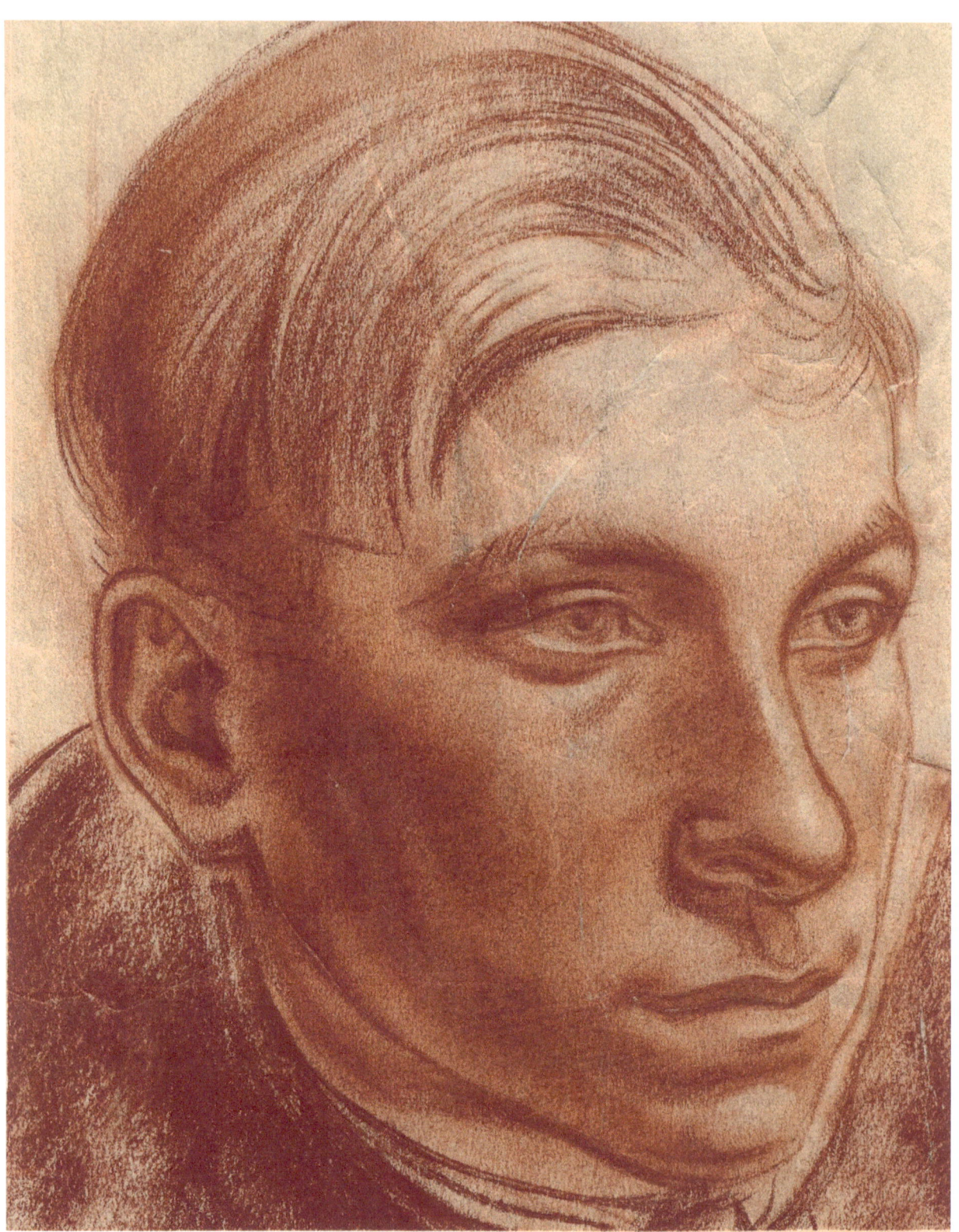

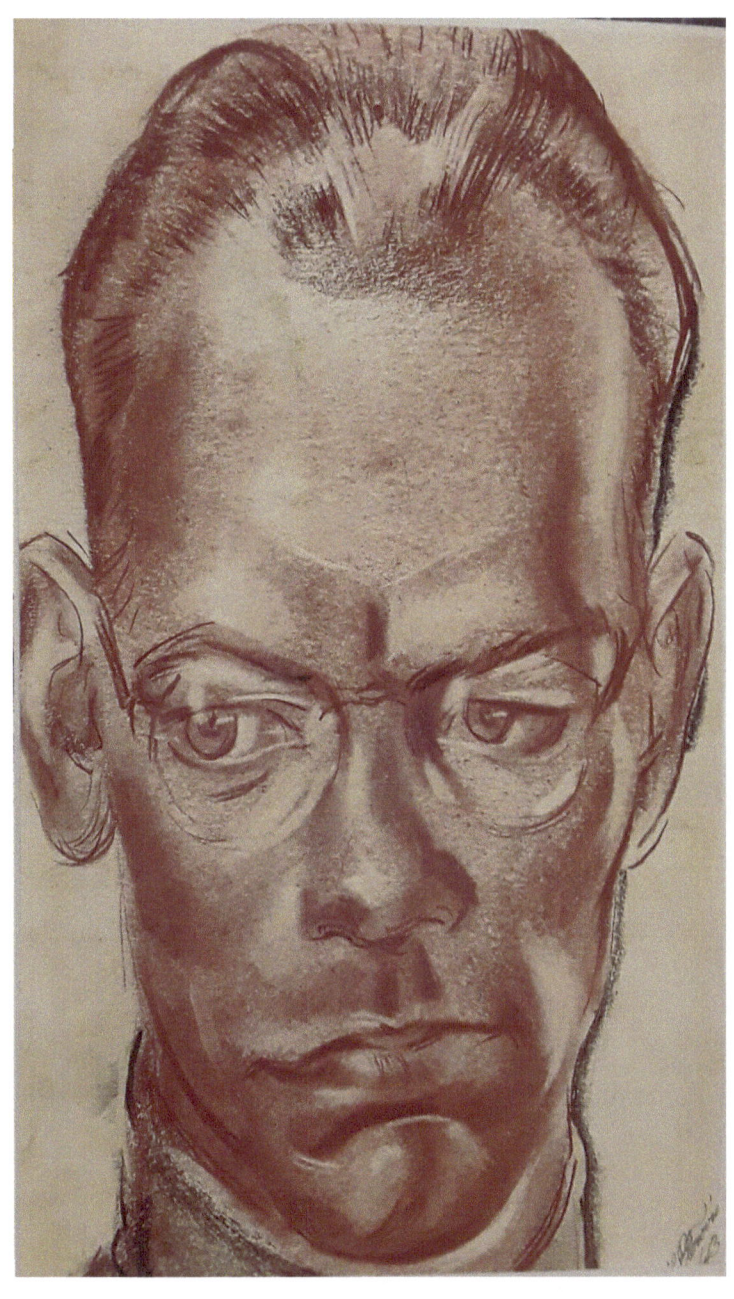

Untitled (Male with Glasses)   charcoal on paper   15 x 9.5"   1943
collection of the Eterovich family

Facing page: *Untitled (Depression Boy)*   charcoal on paper   8.5 x 7.5"   1932
collection of the Eterovich family

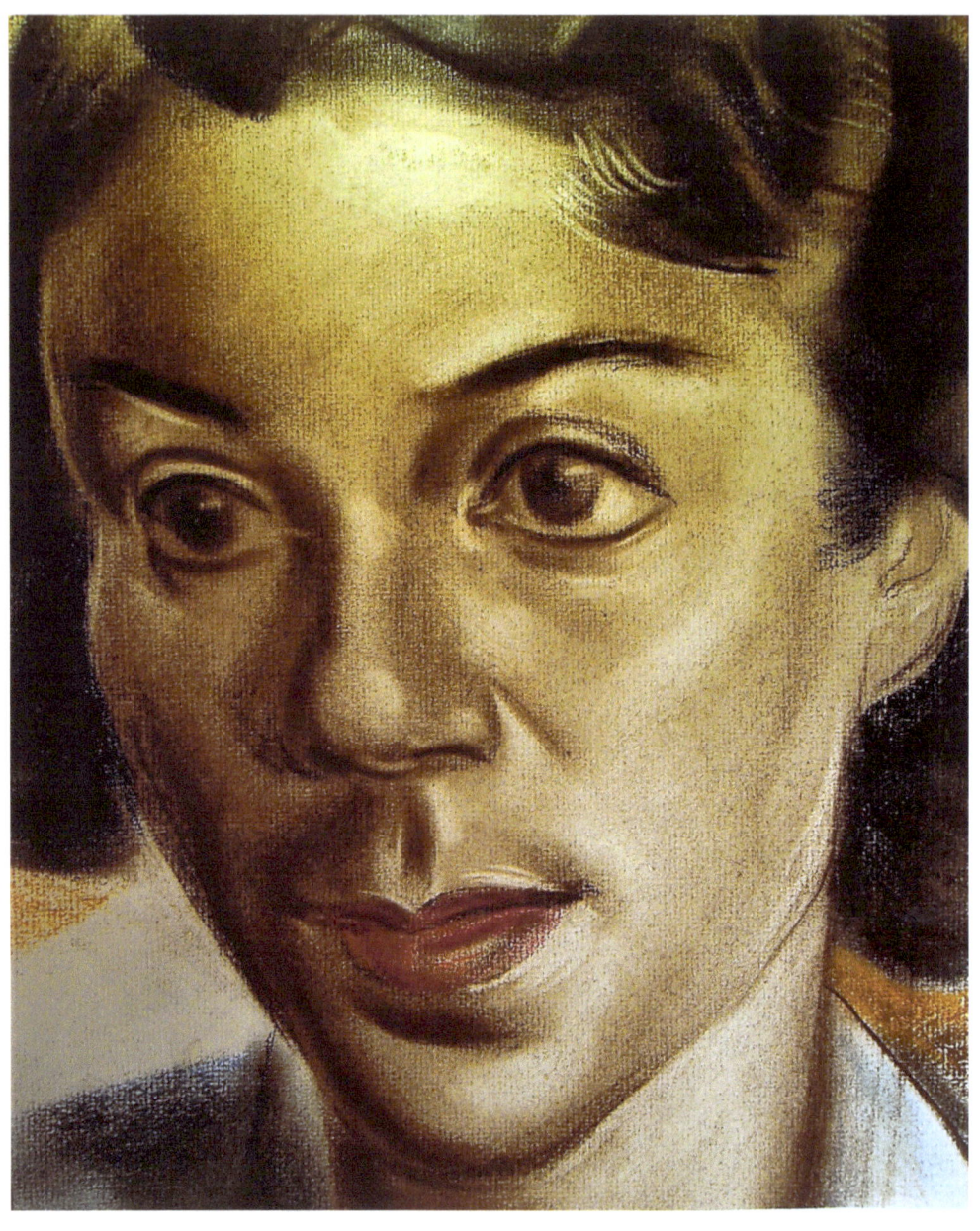

Untitled (portrait of a woman) pastel on paper 12.5 x 10.25" 1938
collection of the Eterovich family

Facing page: *Brother can You Spare a Dime?* charcoal on paper 11 x 9" 1938
collection of the Eterovich family

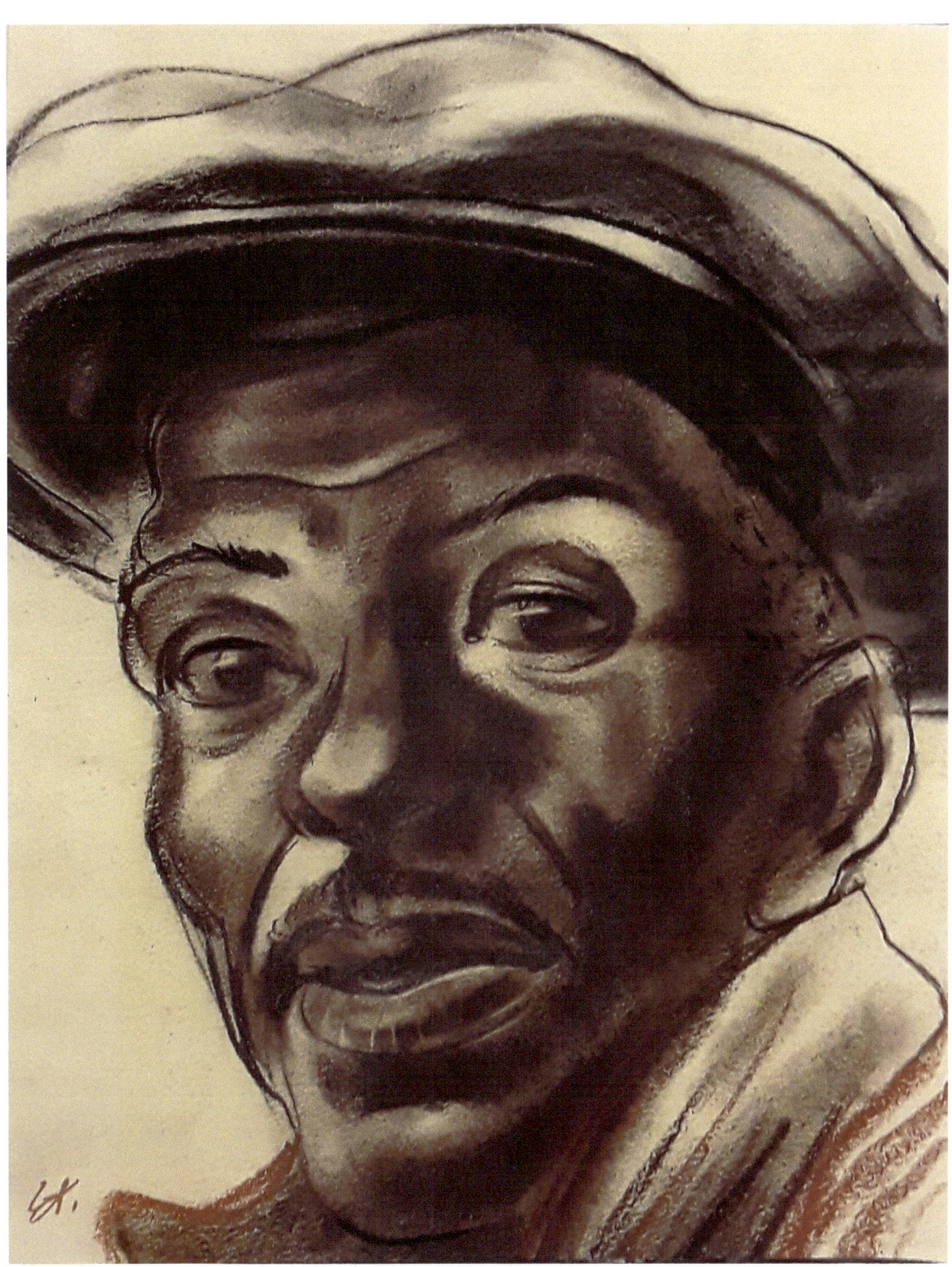

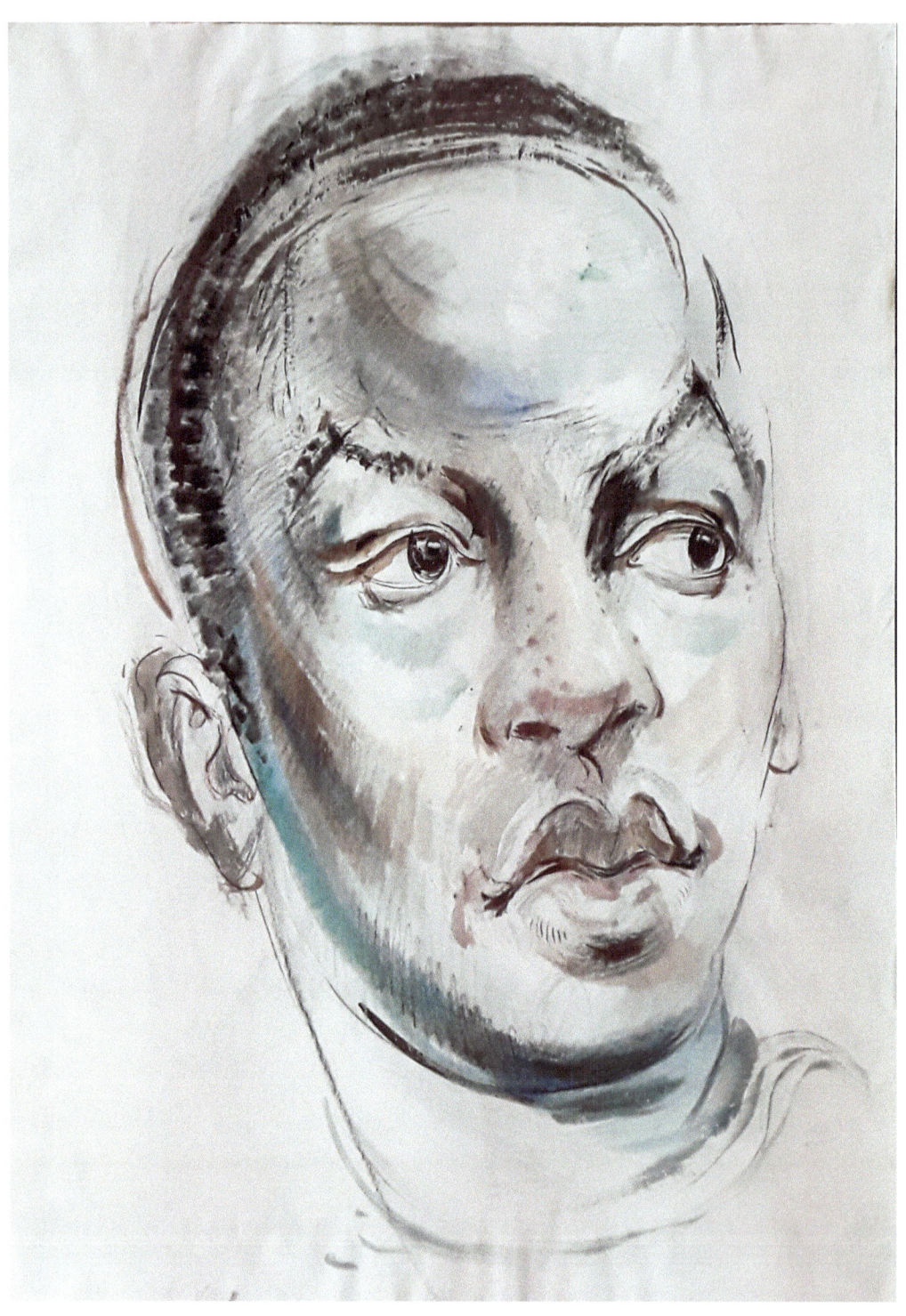

Untitled watercolor and pencil on paper   36 x 24"   1975
collection of the Eterovich family

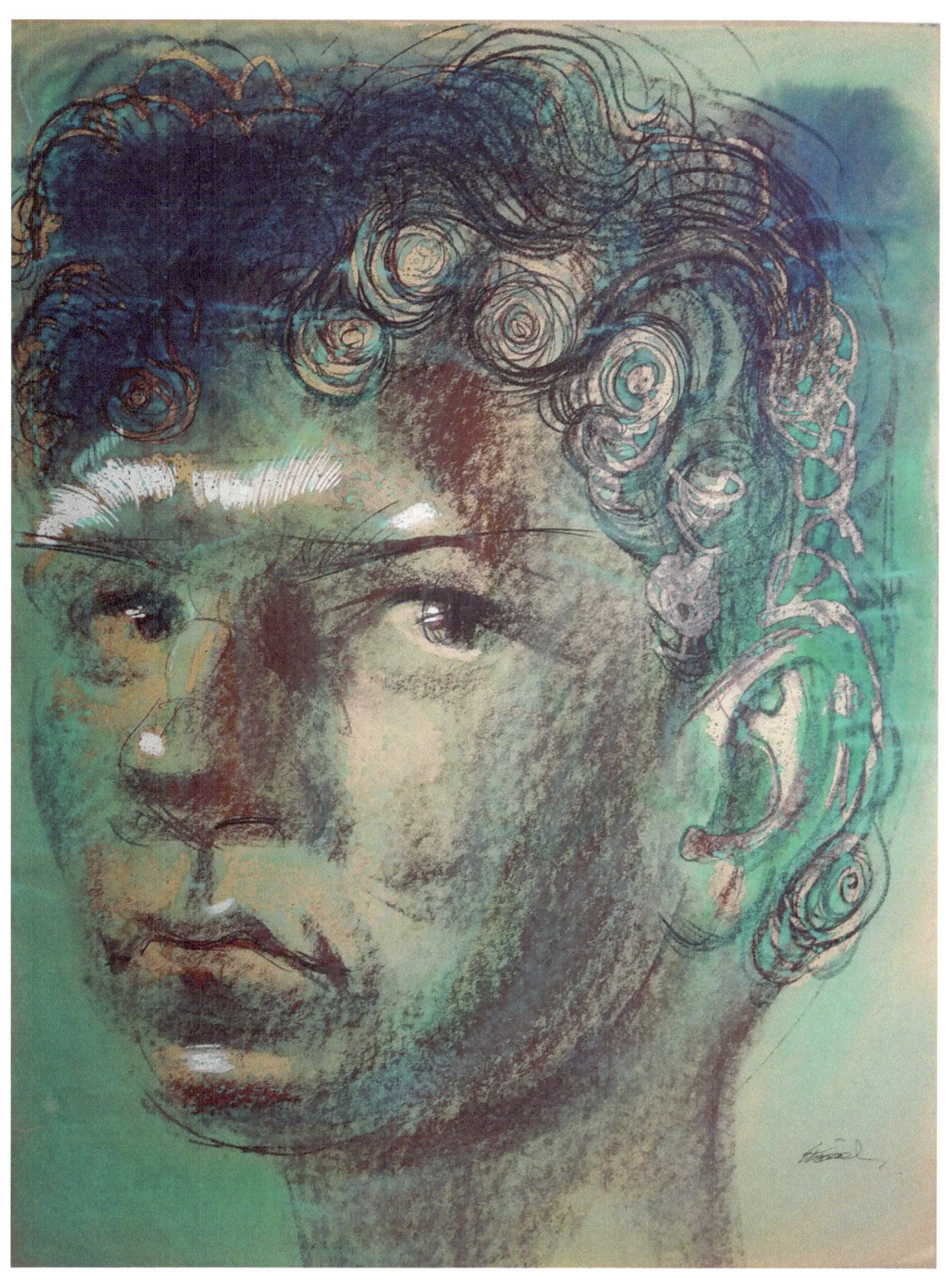

Green, Curly Haired Boy   mixed media on paper   36 x 24"   date unknown
collection of the Eterovich family

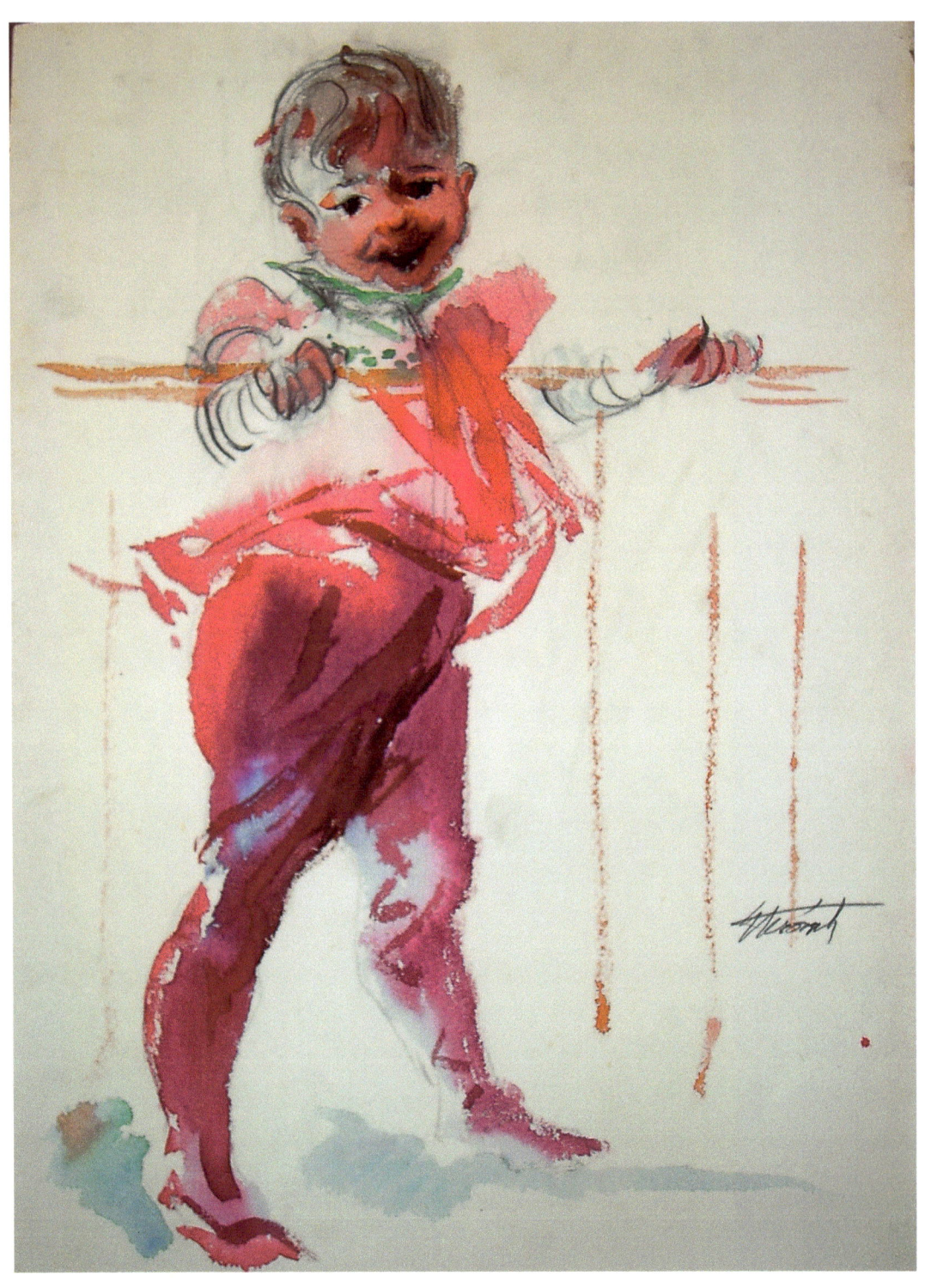

Karen, Standing watercolor on paper 36 x 24" 1961
collection of Karen Eterovich

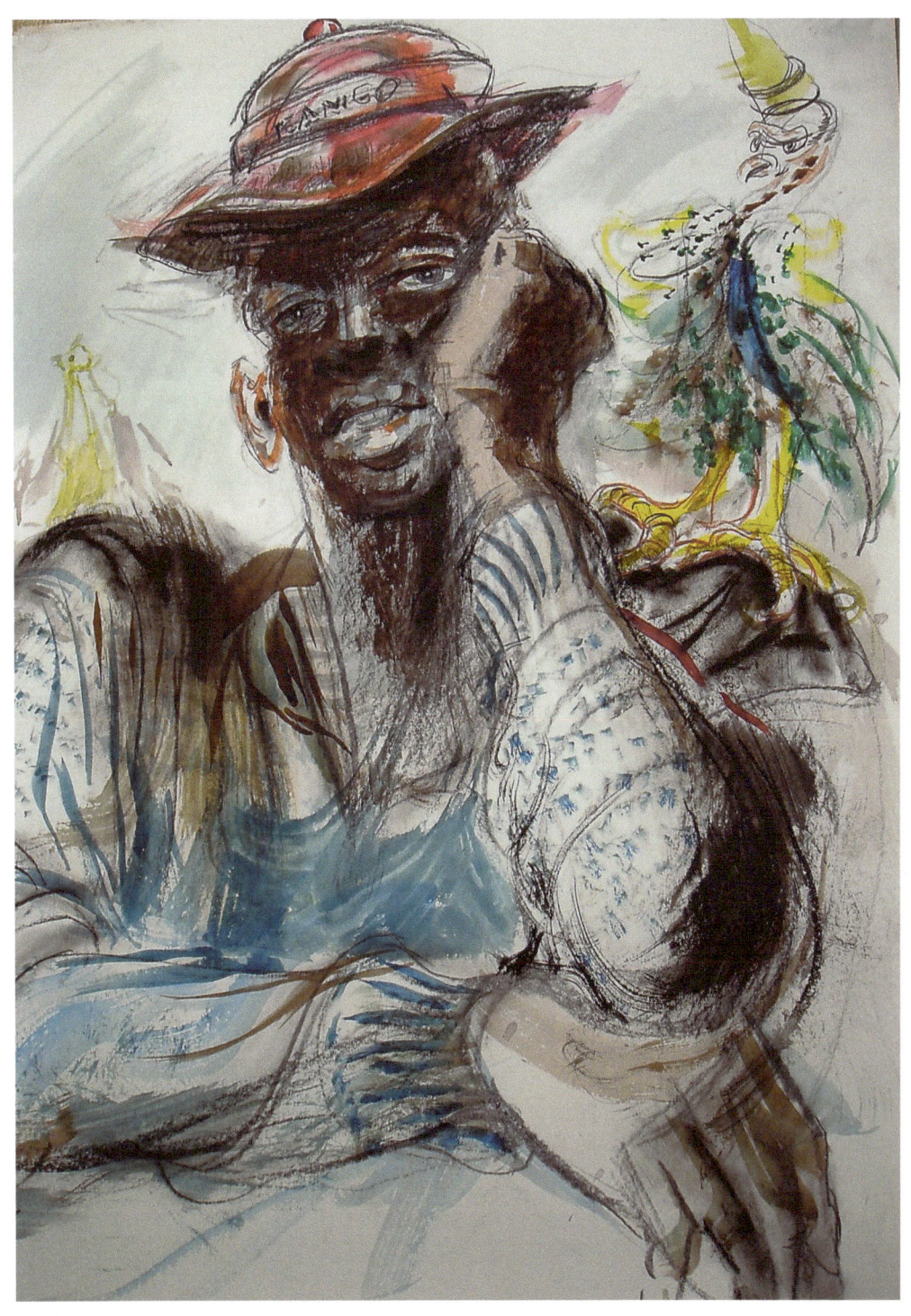

Tango Man   mixed media on paper   36 x 24"   date unknown
collection of the Eterovich family

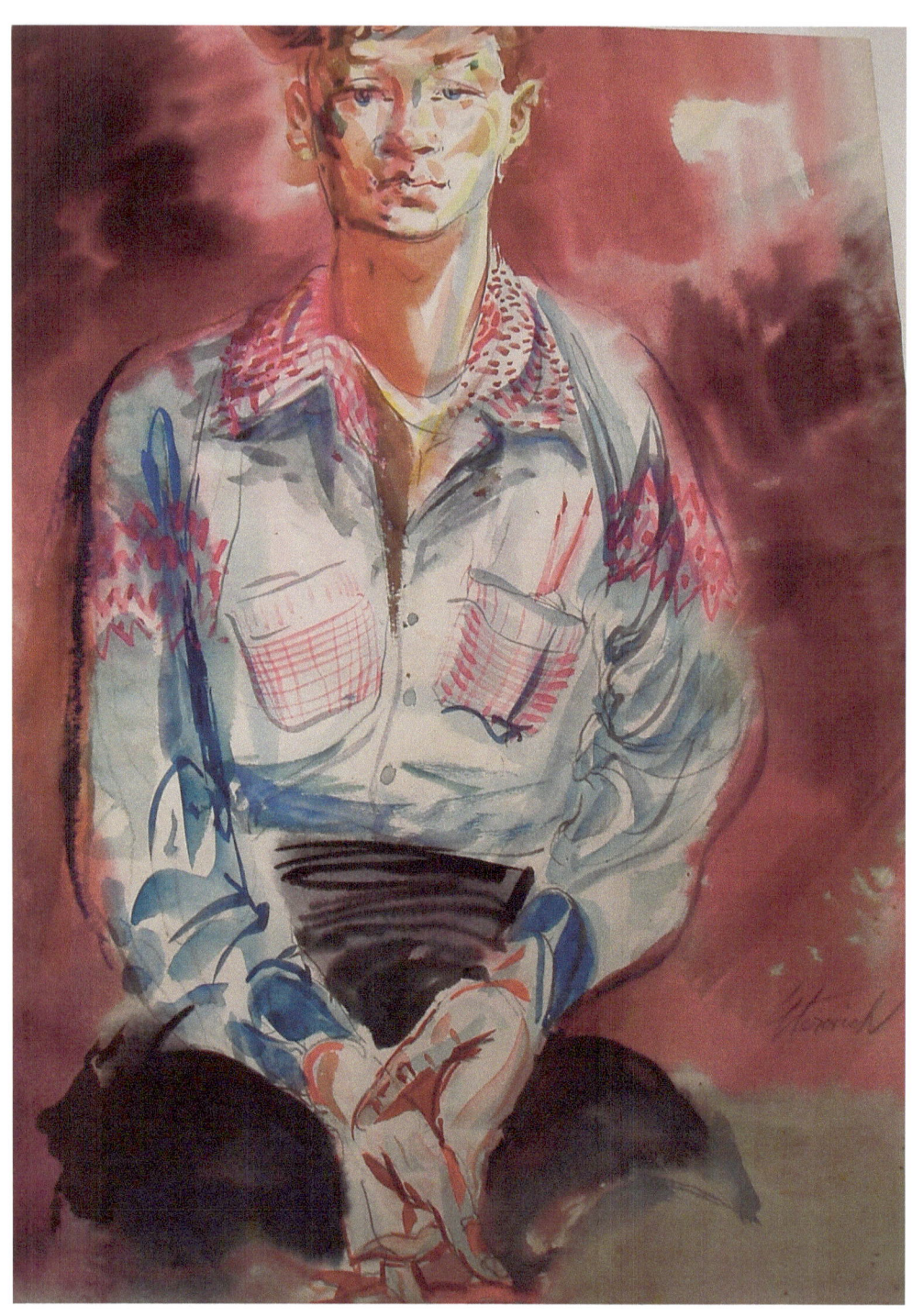

Pensive watercolor on paper 20 x 15" circa 1960's
collection of the Eterovich family

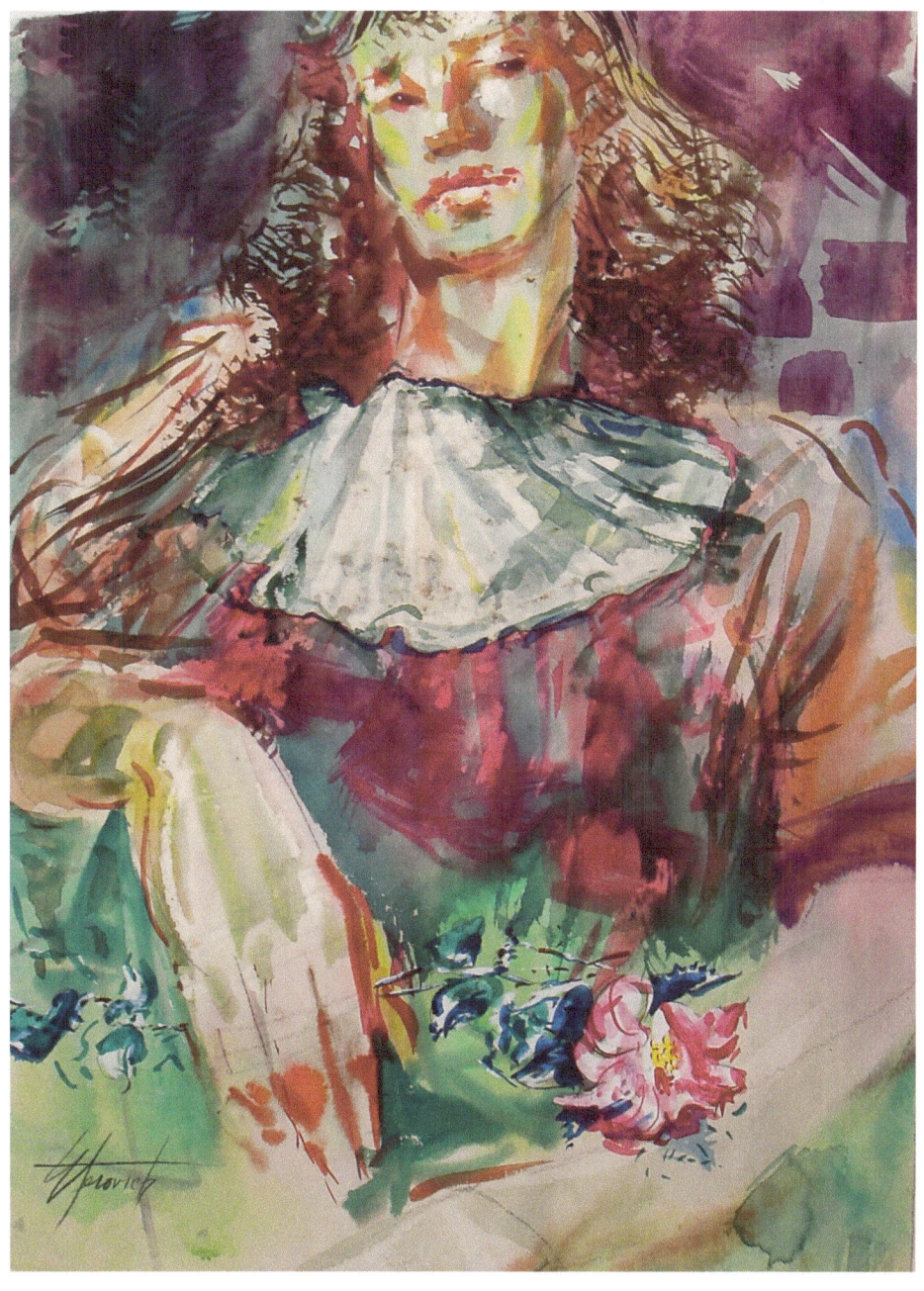

The Rose watercolor on paper 20 x 15" circa 1960's
collection of the Eterovich family

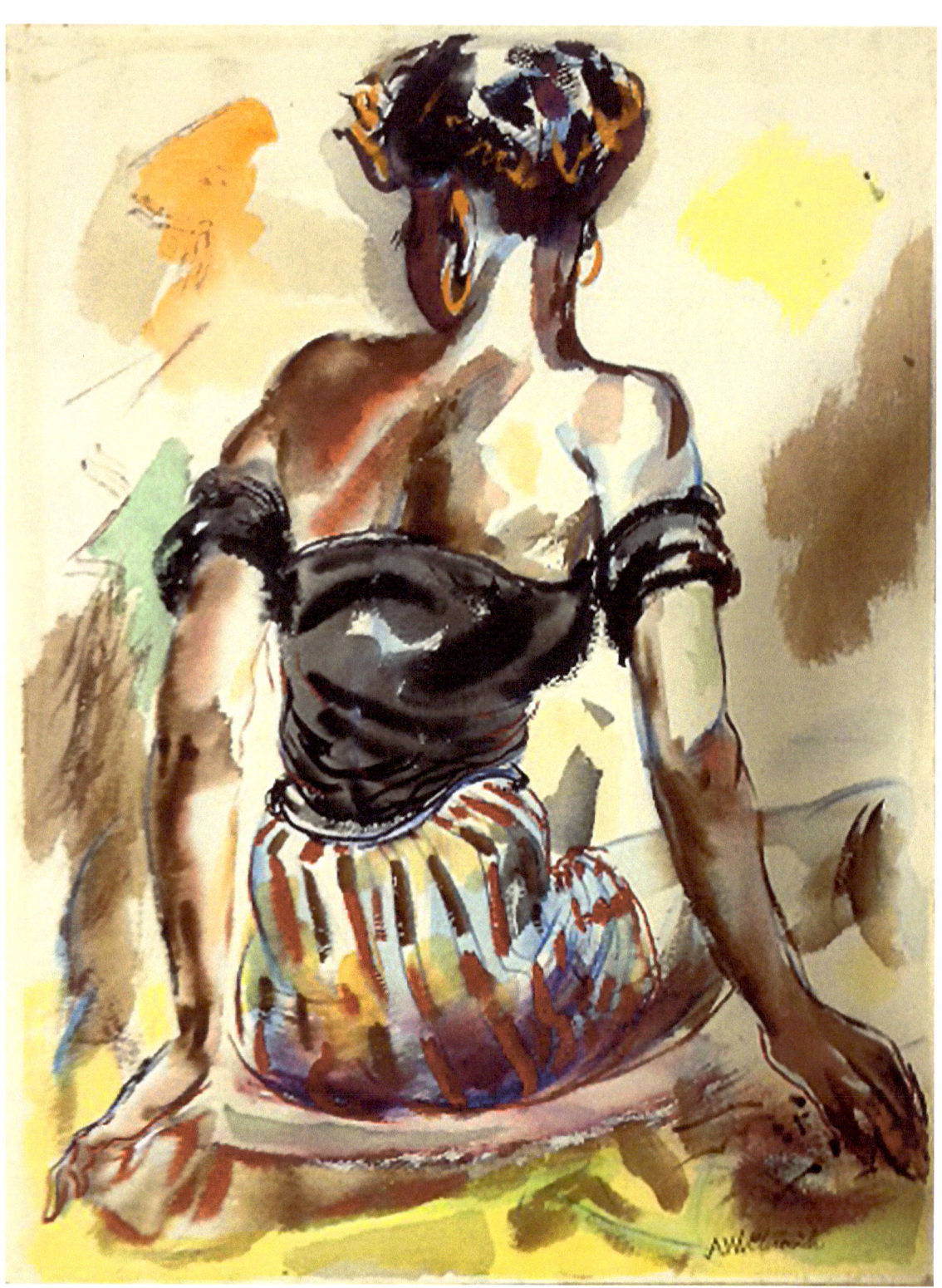

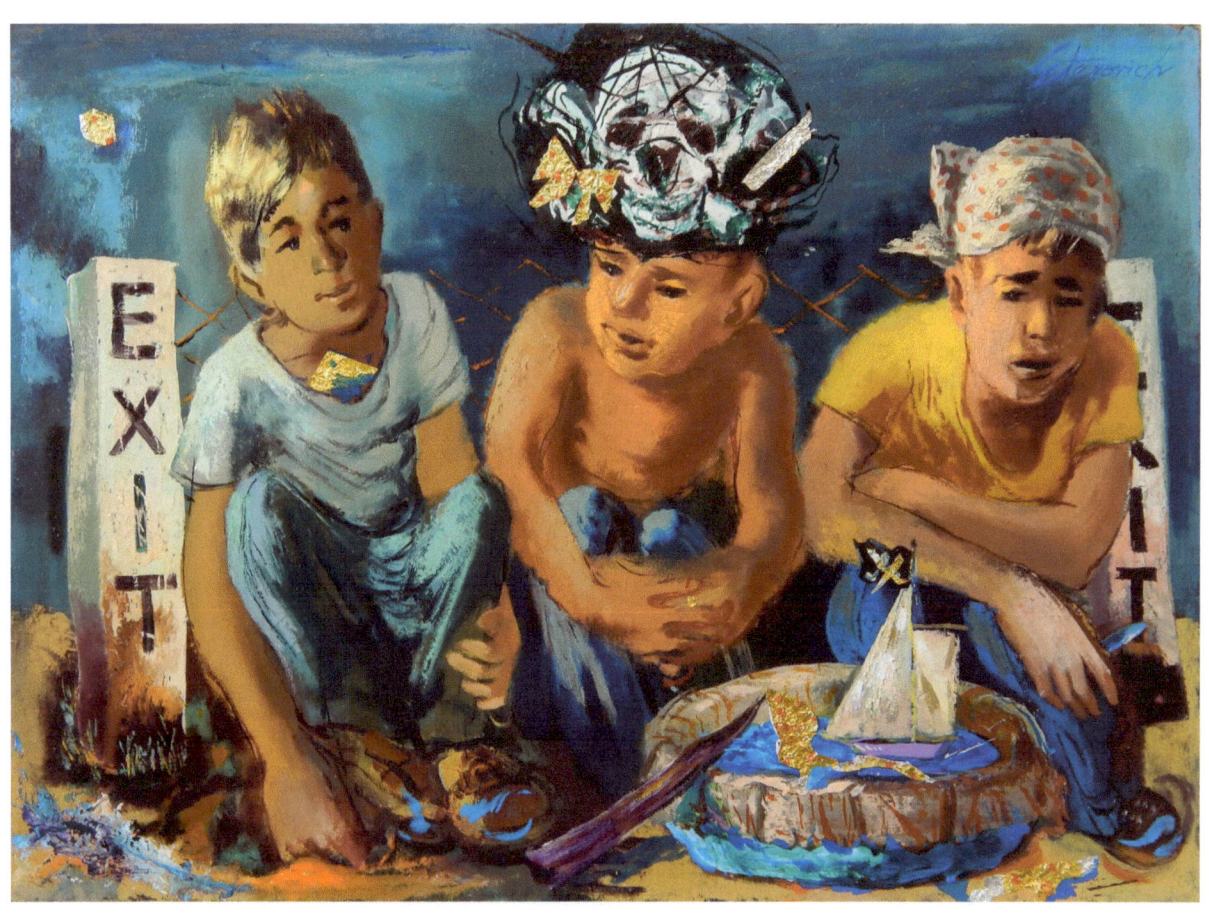

Young Pirates oil on Masonite 19.5 x 27.5" 1962
collection of ARTneo, Gift of Alice Eterovich and Karen Eterovich Maguire

Facing page: *Untitled (woman in striped shorts)* watercolor and pencil on paper 23 x 17.5" circa 1945
collection of the AAWR, Gift of Alice Eterovich and Karen Eterovich Maquire

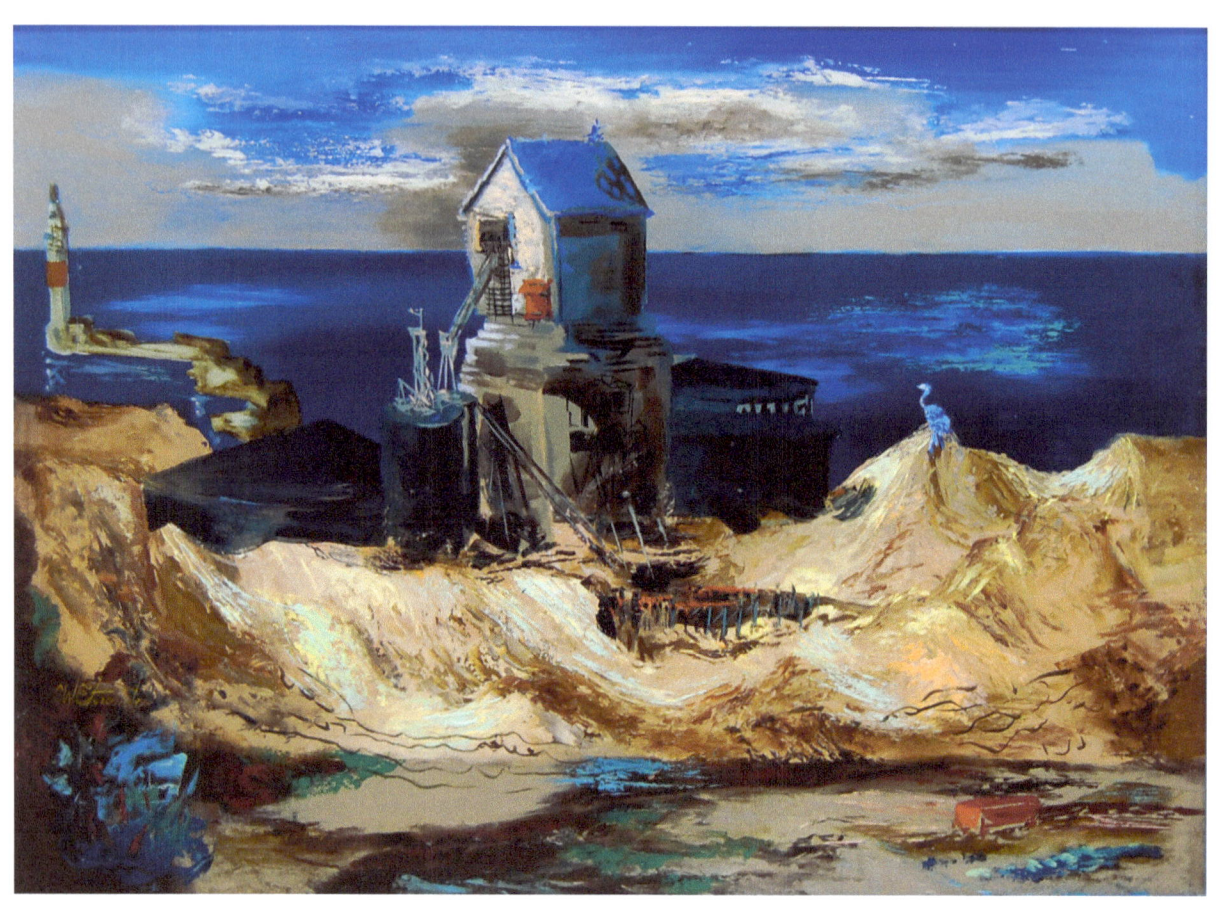

The Dunes oil on Masonite 30 x 40" 1940
collection of the Eterovich family

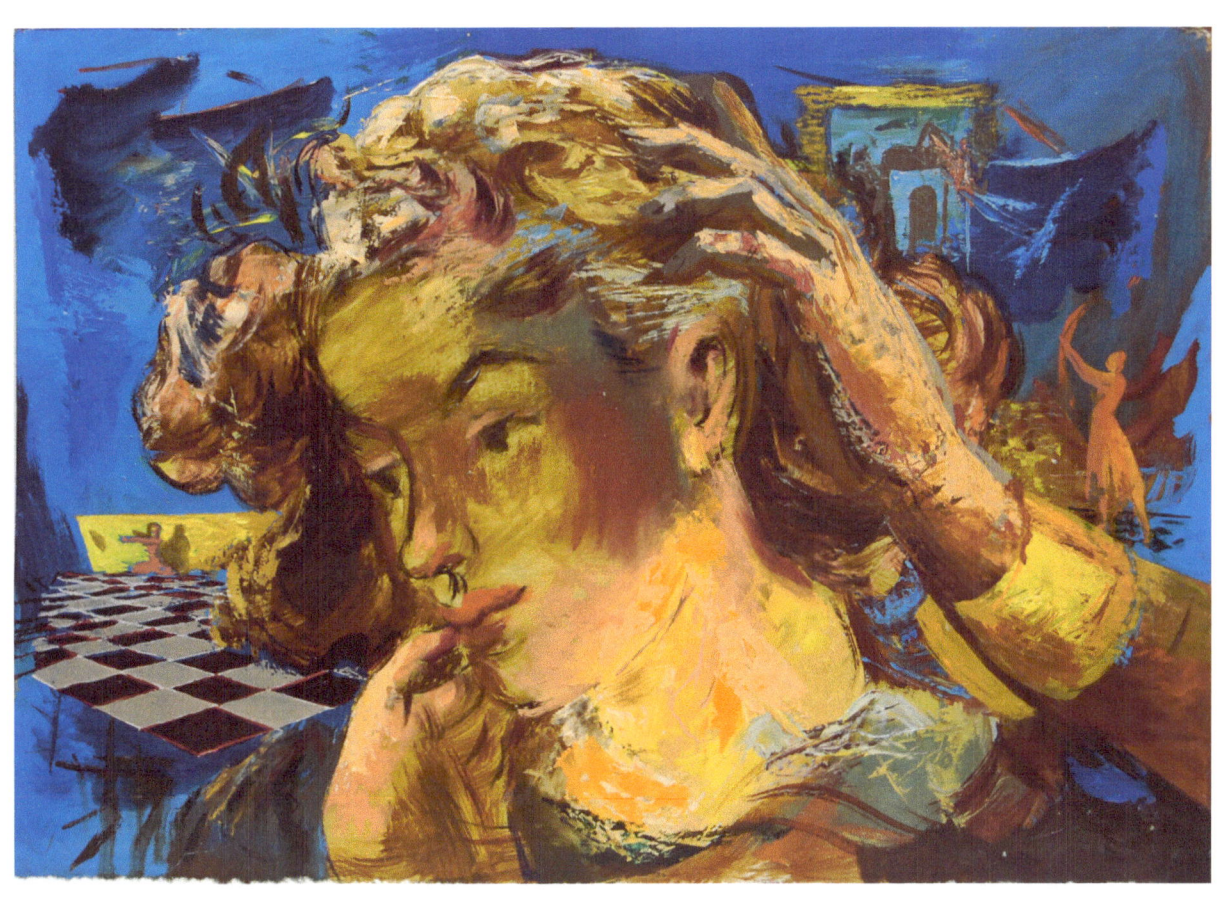

The Choreographer oil on Masonite 15.5 x 22.25" 1946
collection of AAWR, Gift of Alice Eterovich and Karen Eterovich Maguire

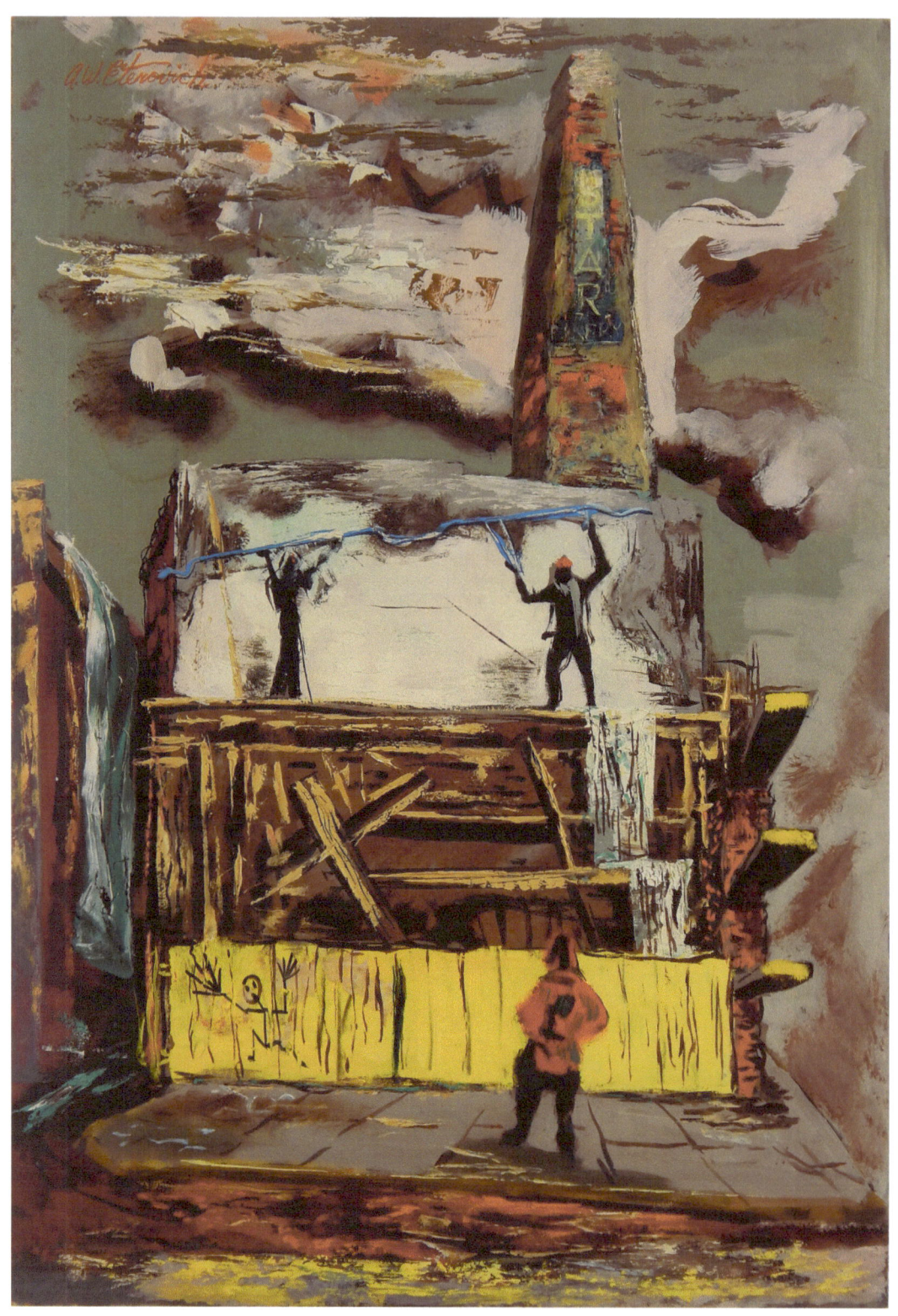

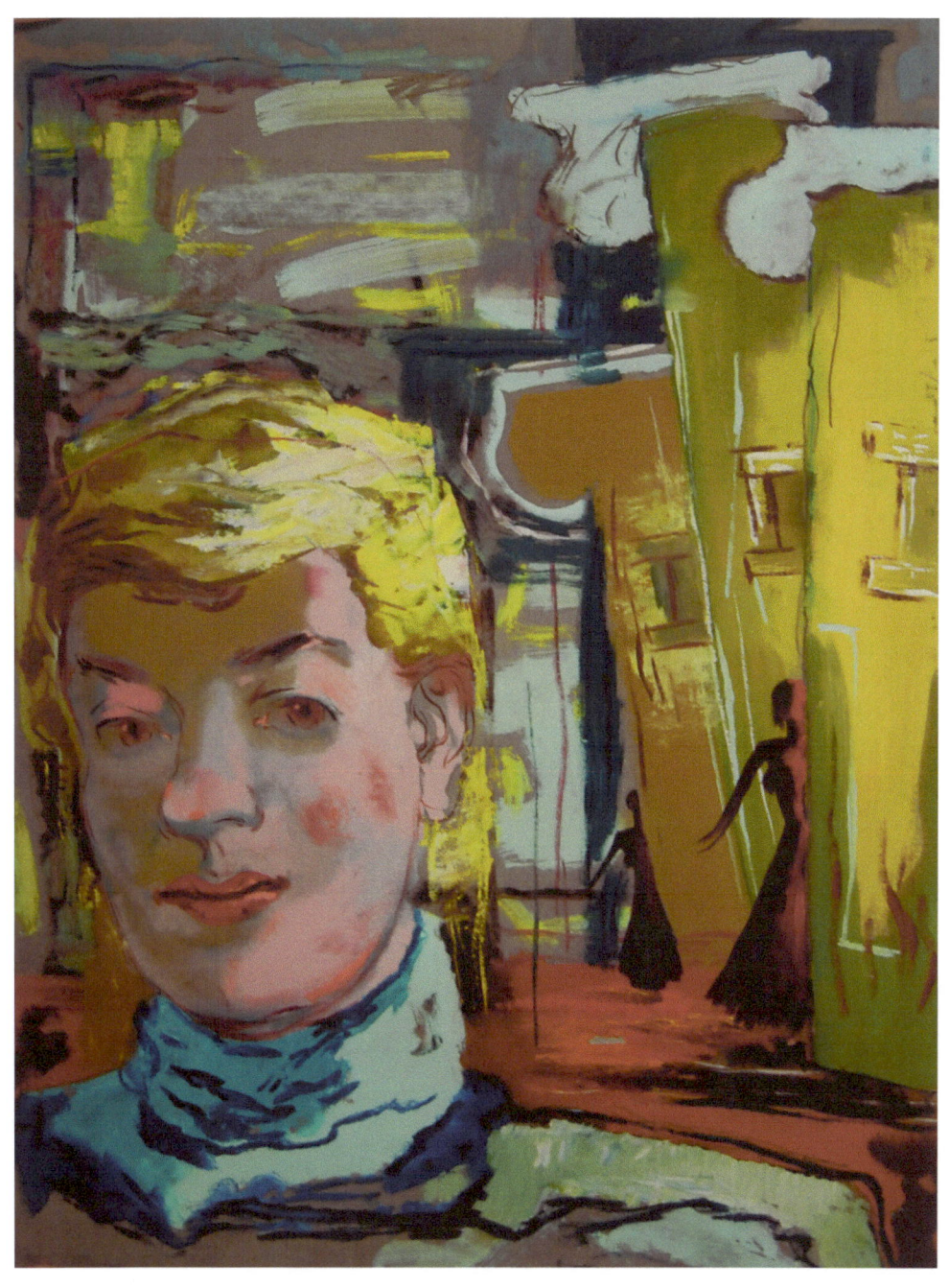

Untitled (blonde portrait) oil on Masonite   24 x 17"   1949
collection of the AAWR, Gift of Alice Eterovich and Karen Eterovich Maguire

Facing page: *Effacement* oil on Masonite   27.5 x 19.5"   1948
collection of ARTneo, Gift of Alice Eterovich and Karen Eterovich Maguire

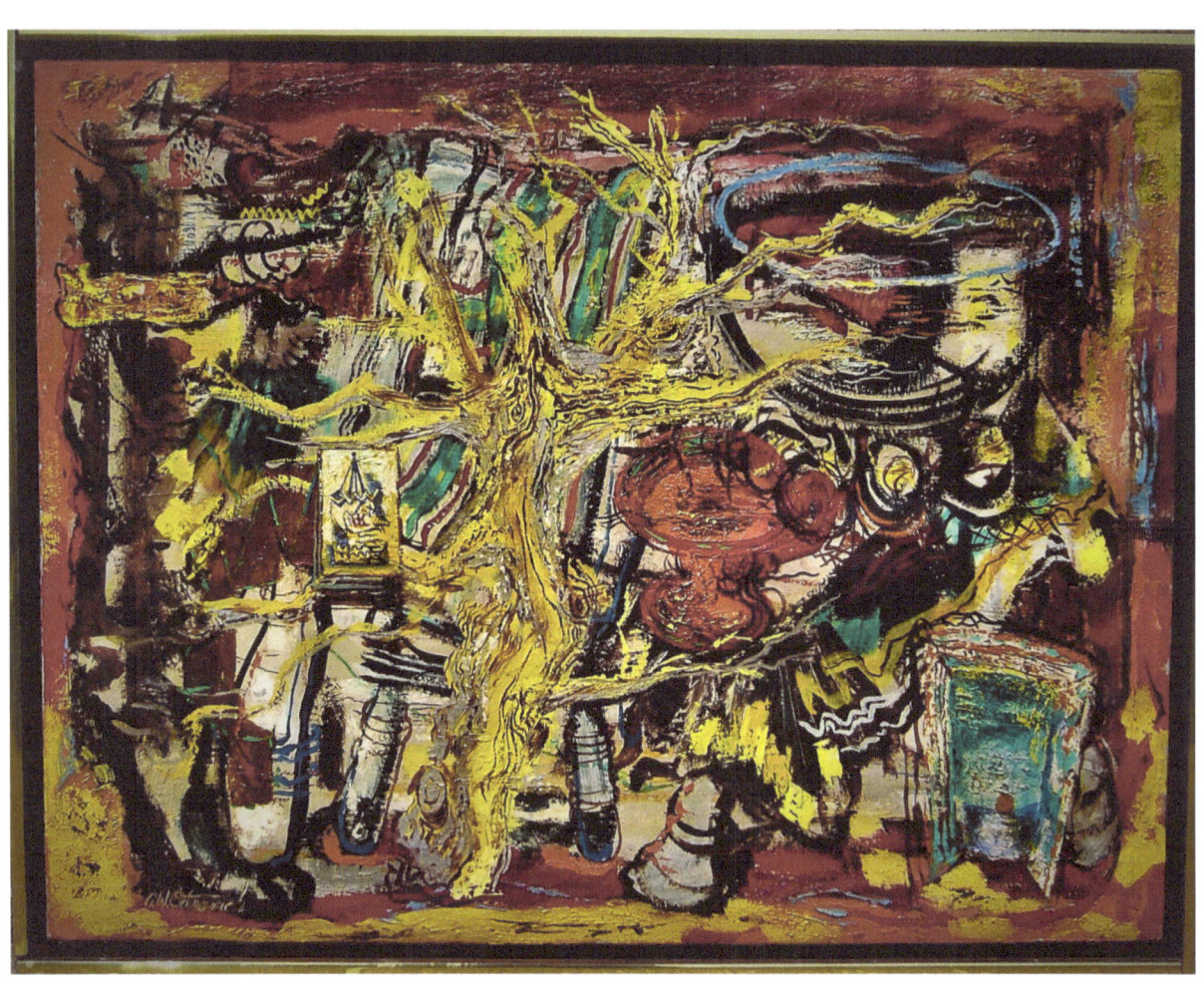

Table Charade oil on canvas 30 x 40" 1951
collection of the Eterovich family

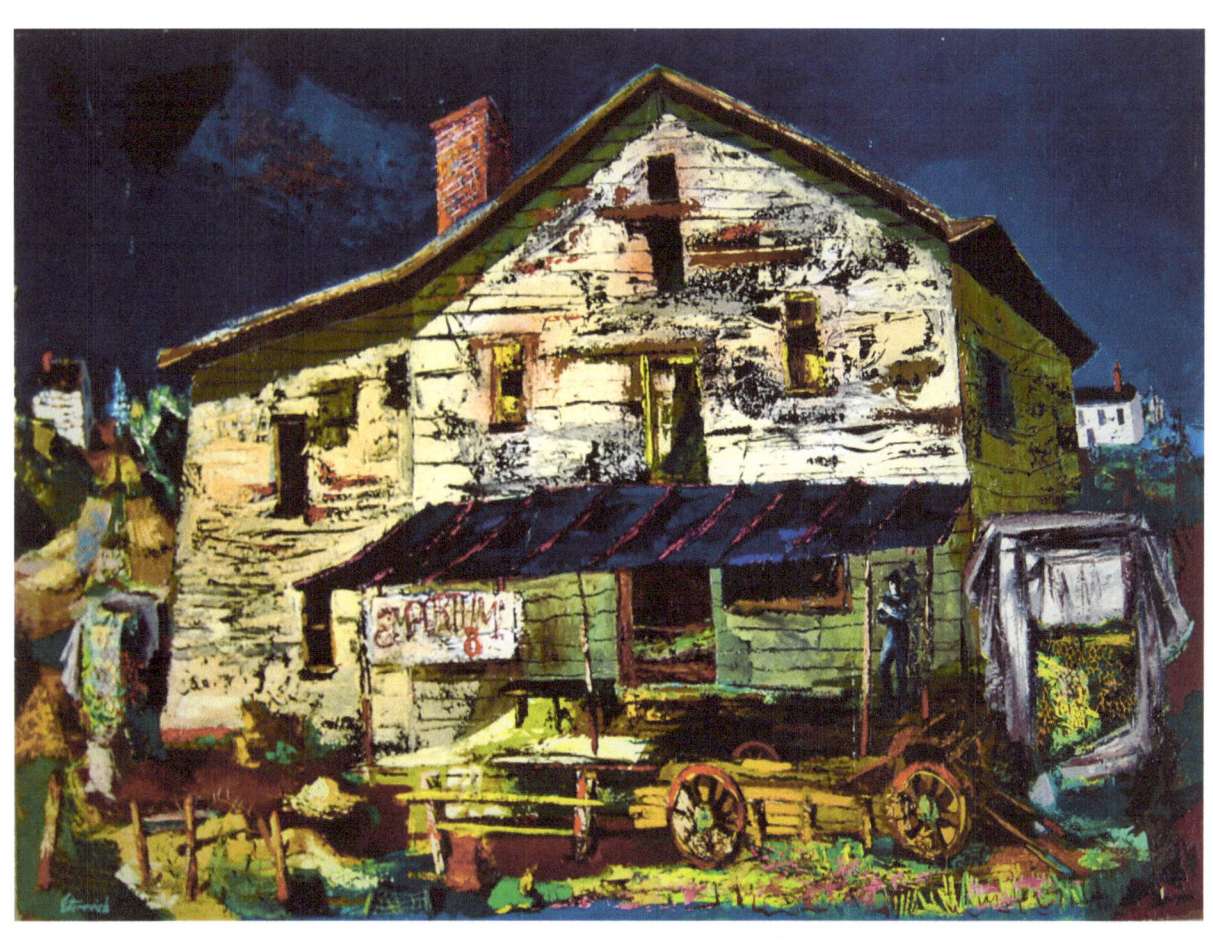

Regal Decline oil on Masonite 30 x 48"   1956
collection of the AAWR, Gift of Alice Eterovich and Karen Eterovich Maguire

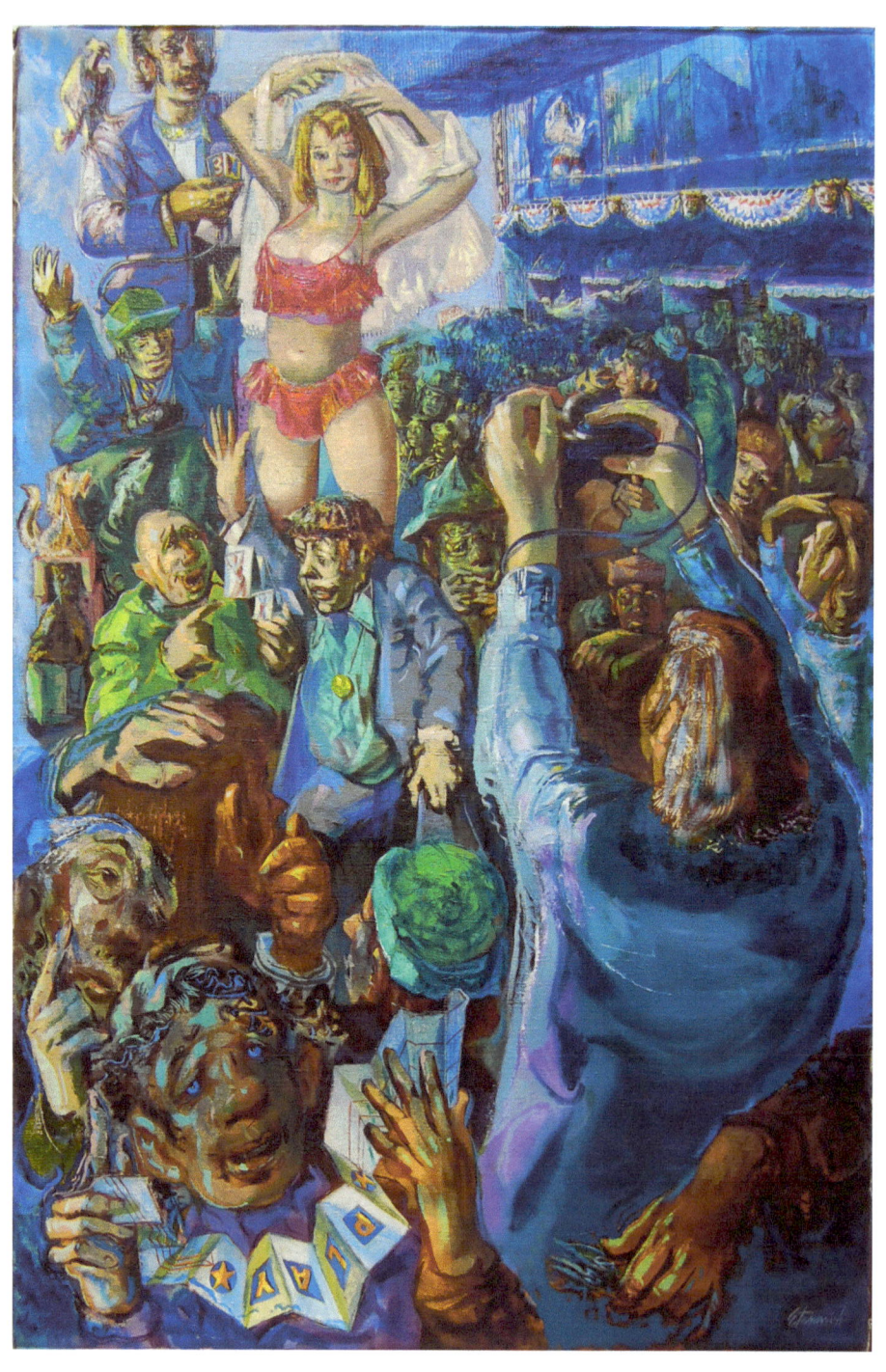

City Visitor oil on canvas 60 x 40" 1976
collection of the AAWR, Gift of Alice Eterovich and Karen Eterovich Maguire

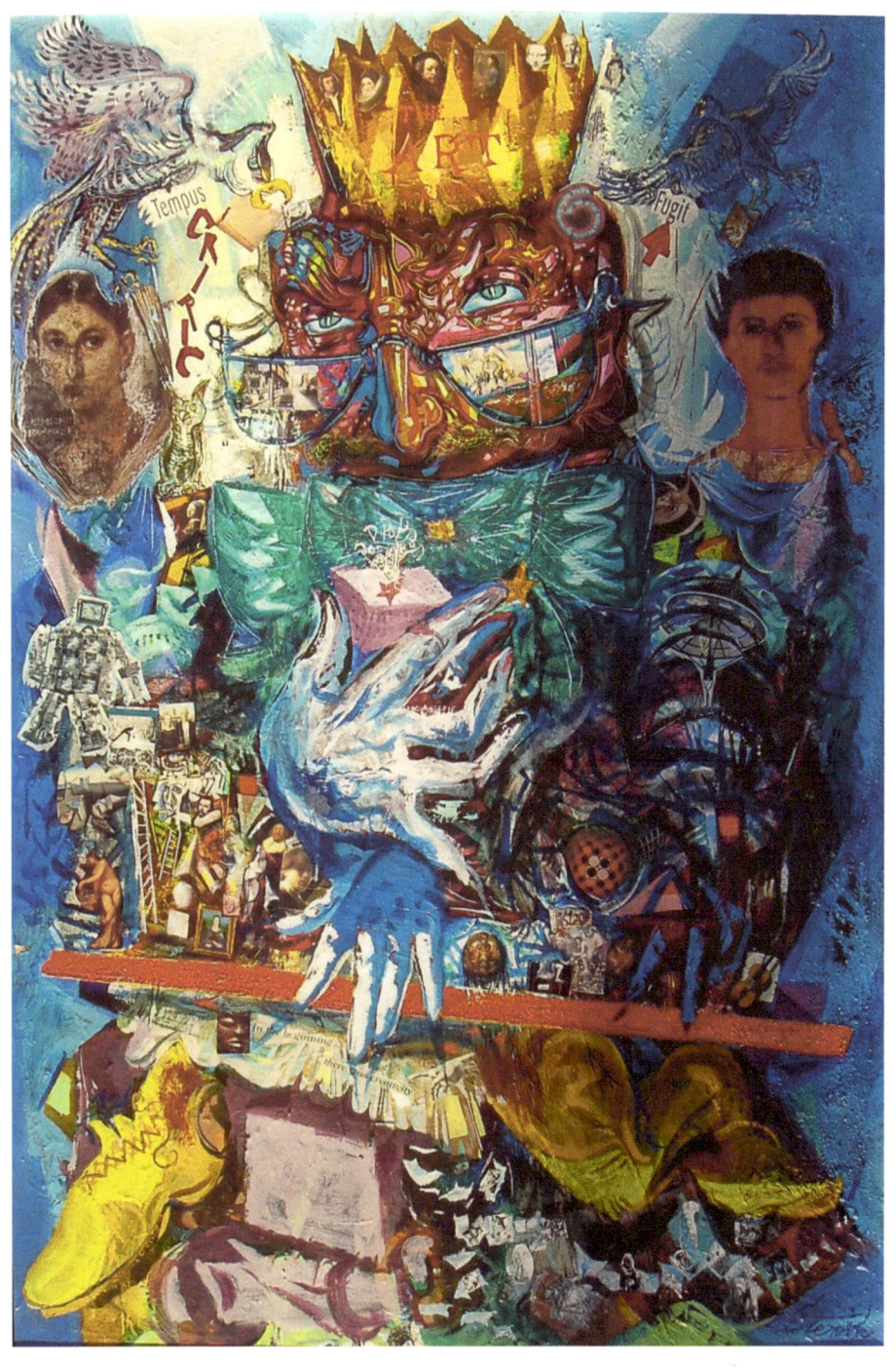

Always Running Art Critic oil on canvas 60 x 40" 1970
collection of the Eterovich family

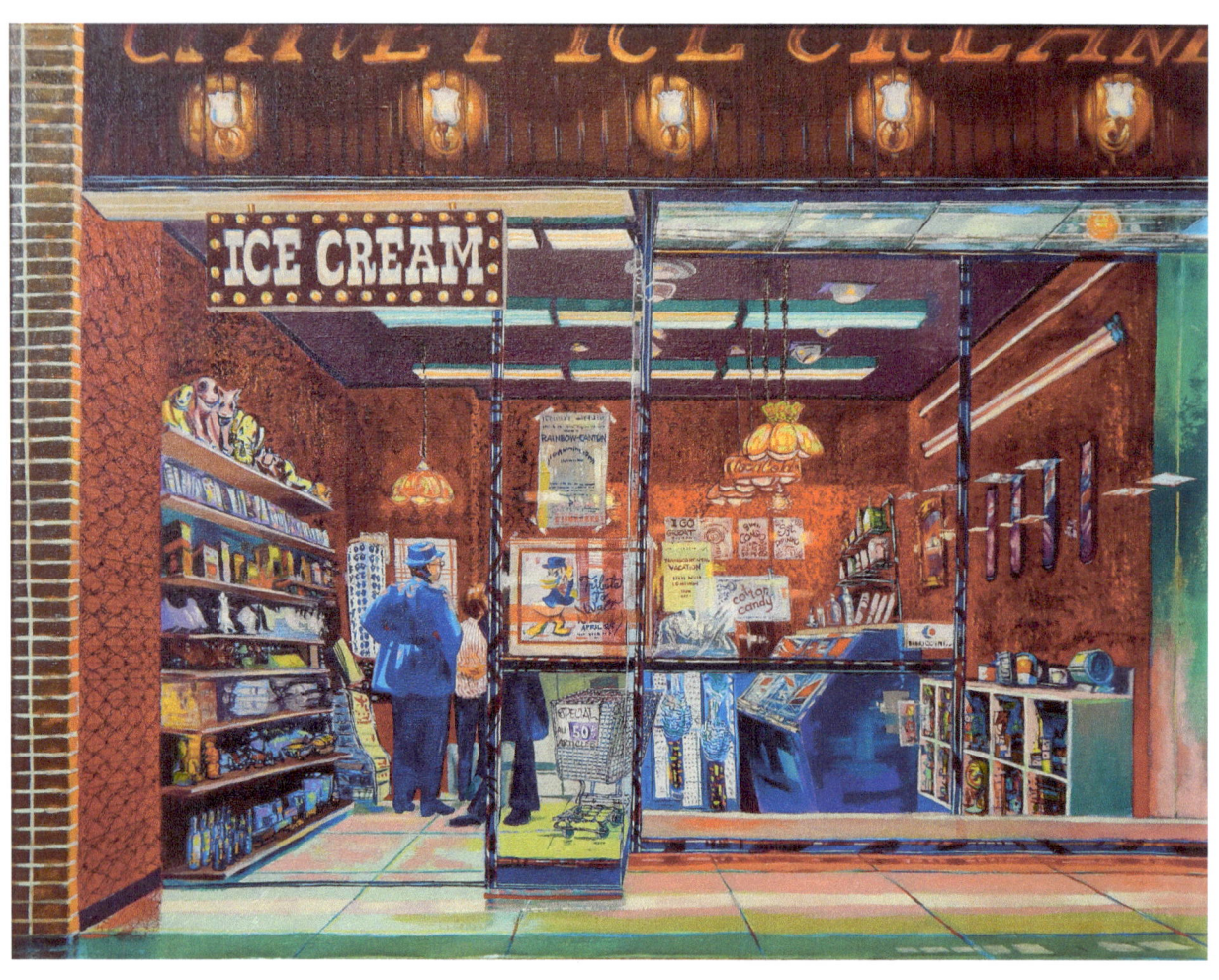

Ice Cream Delights oil on canvas 30 x 40" 1994
collection of ARTneo, Gift of Alice Eterovich and Karen Eterovich Maguire

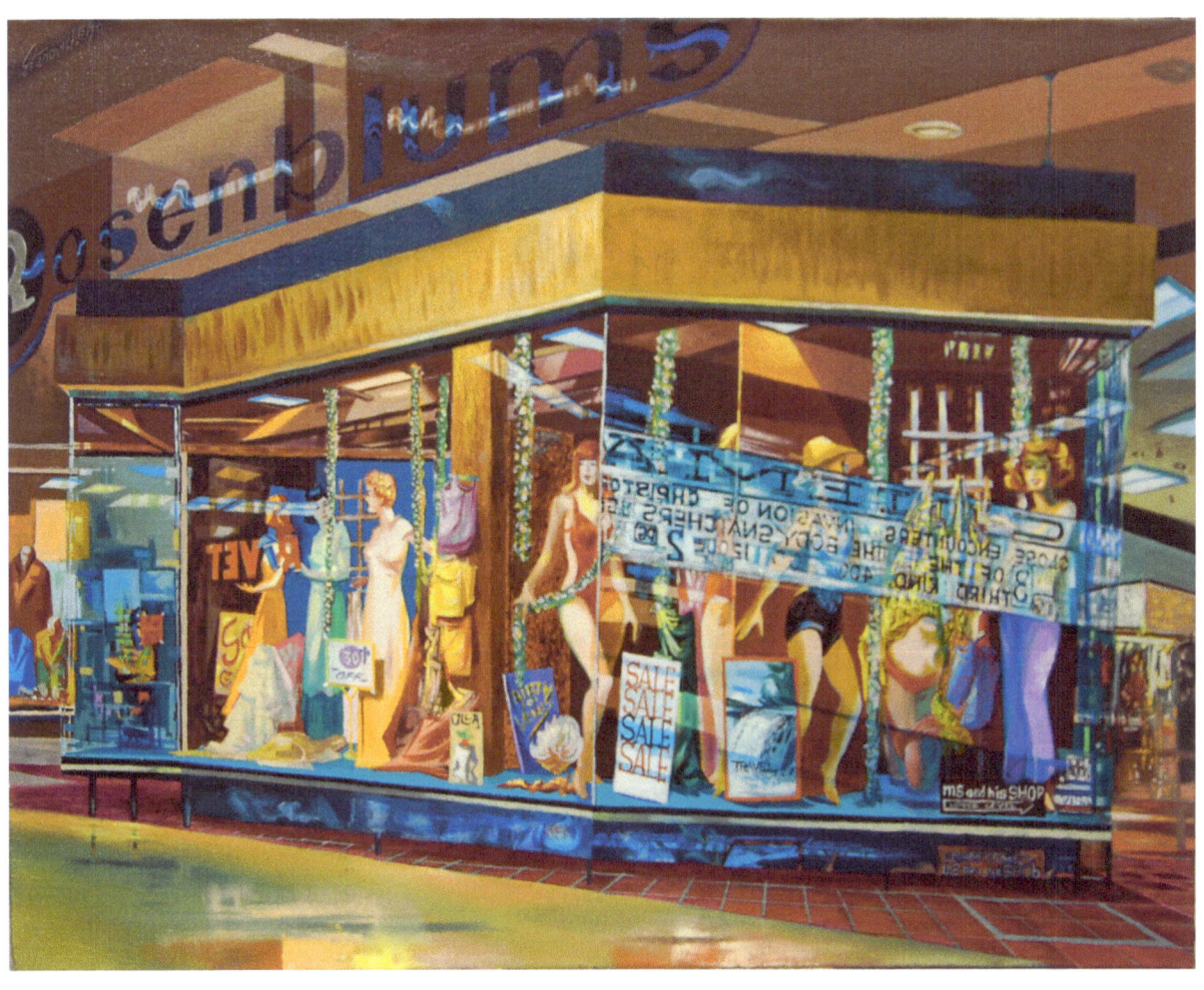

Venus de Mall   oil on linen 30 x 40" 1979
collection of the AAWR, Gift of Alice Eterovich and Karen Eterovich Maguire

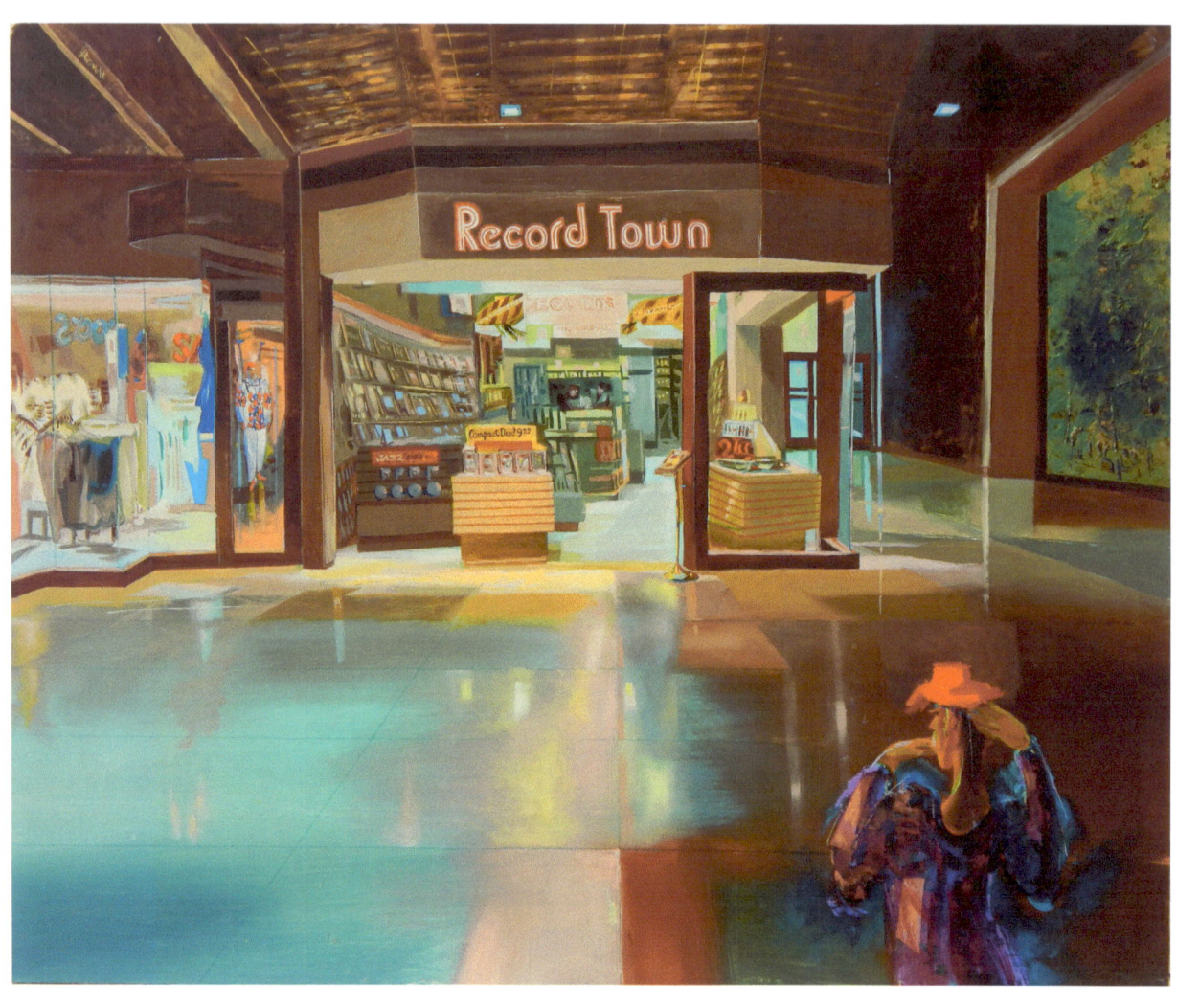

Record Town oil on Masonite   24 x 40" 1977
collection of ARTneo, Gift of Alice Eterovich and Karen Eterovich Maguire

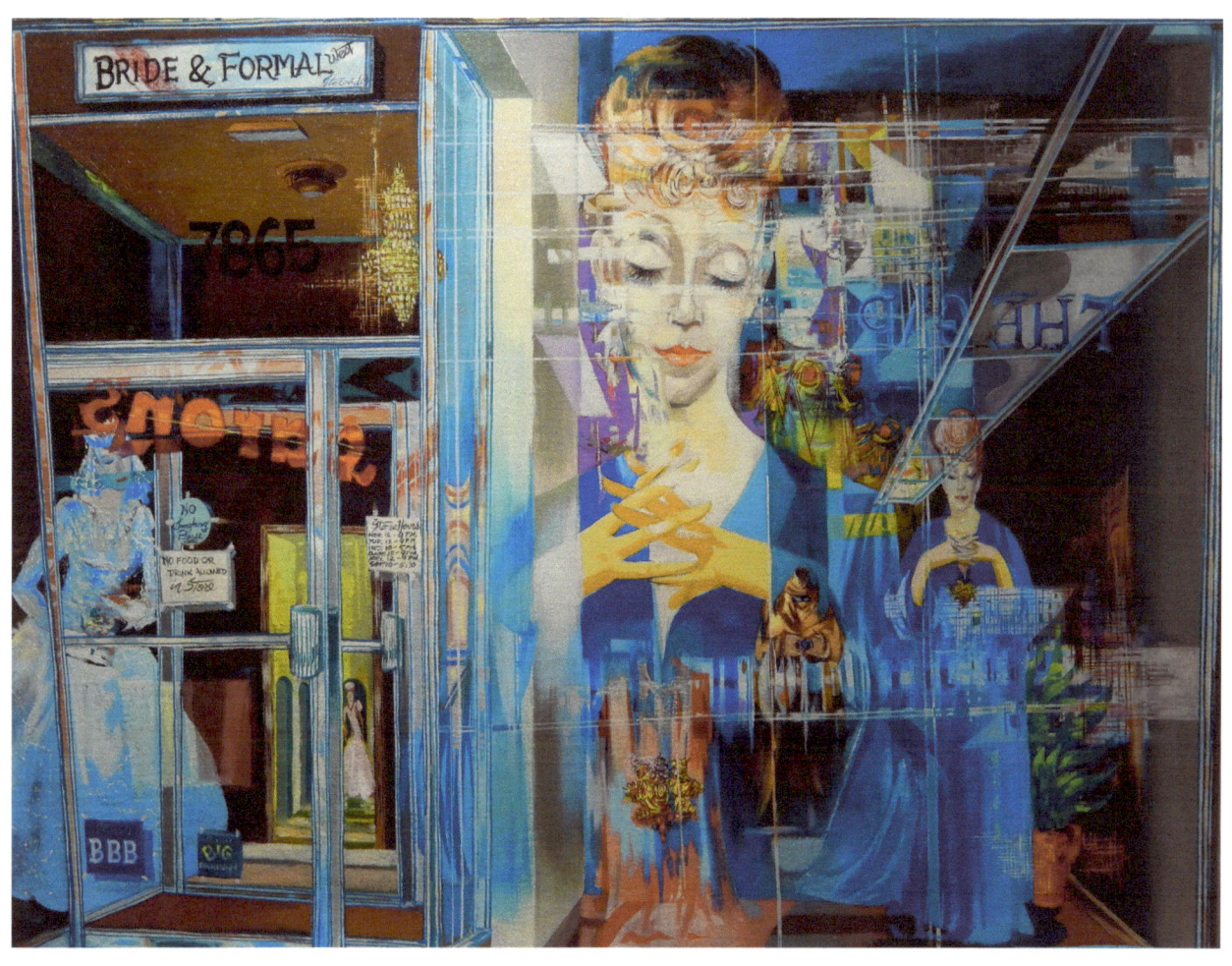

Bride and Formal oil on canvas 30 x 40" 1975
collection of ARTneo, Gift of Alice Eterovich and Karen Eterovich Maguire

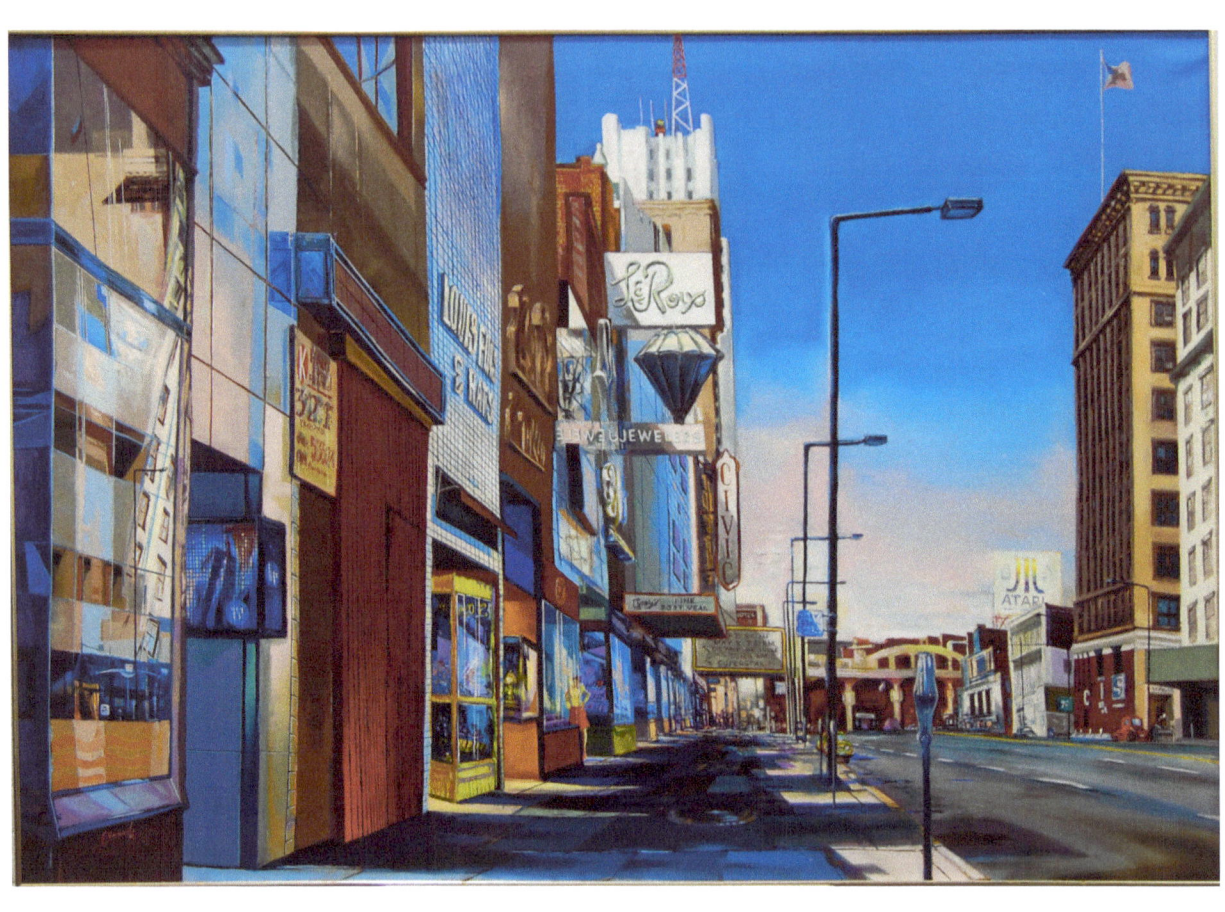

City Reveries oil on canvas 40 x 60" 1983
collection of the AAWR, Gift of Alice Eterovich and Karen Eterovich Maguire

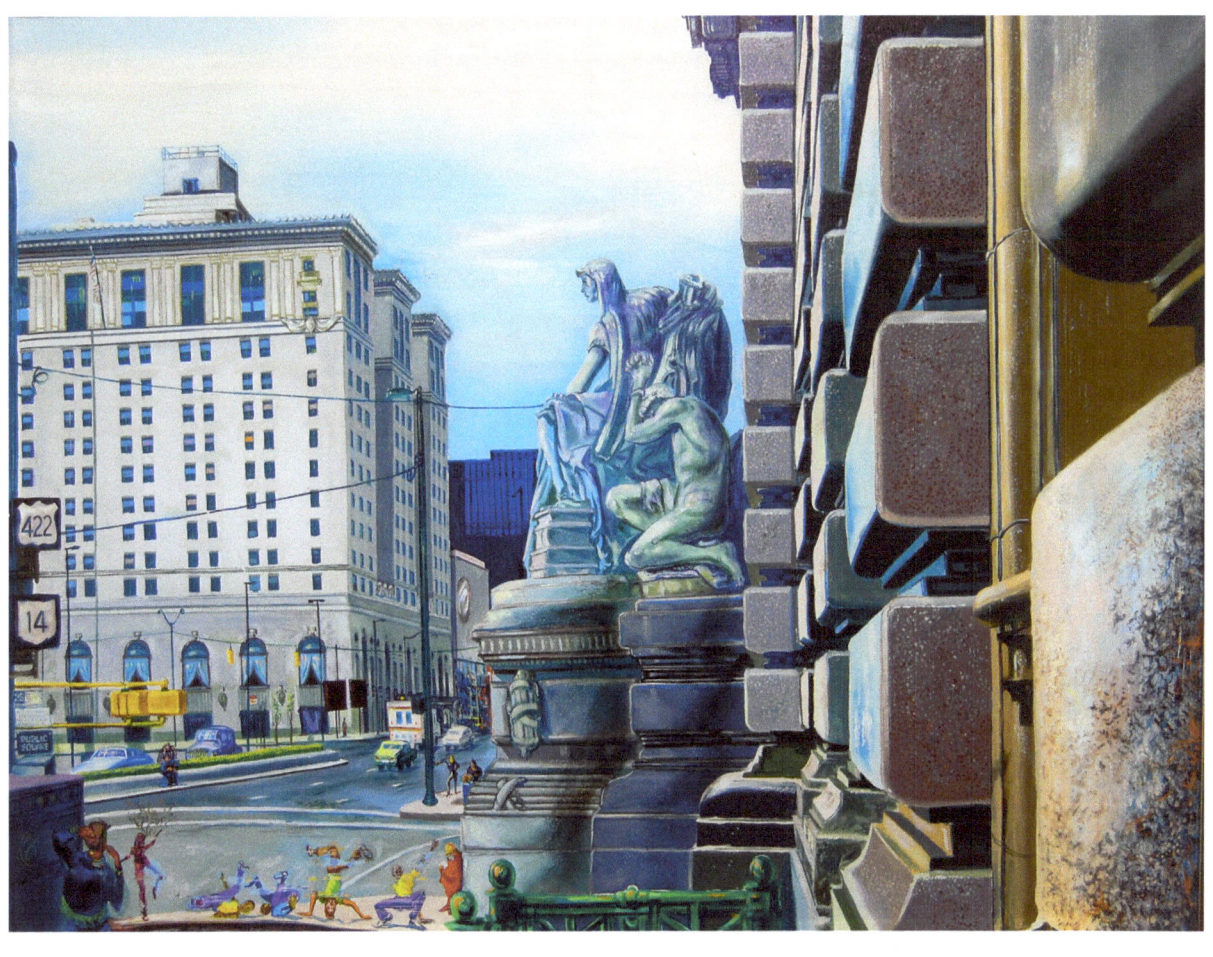

Break Dancers oil on canvas 30 x 40" 1983
collection of the Eterovich family

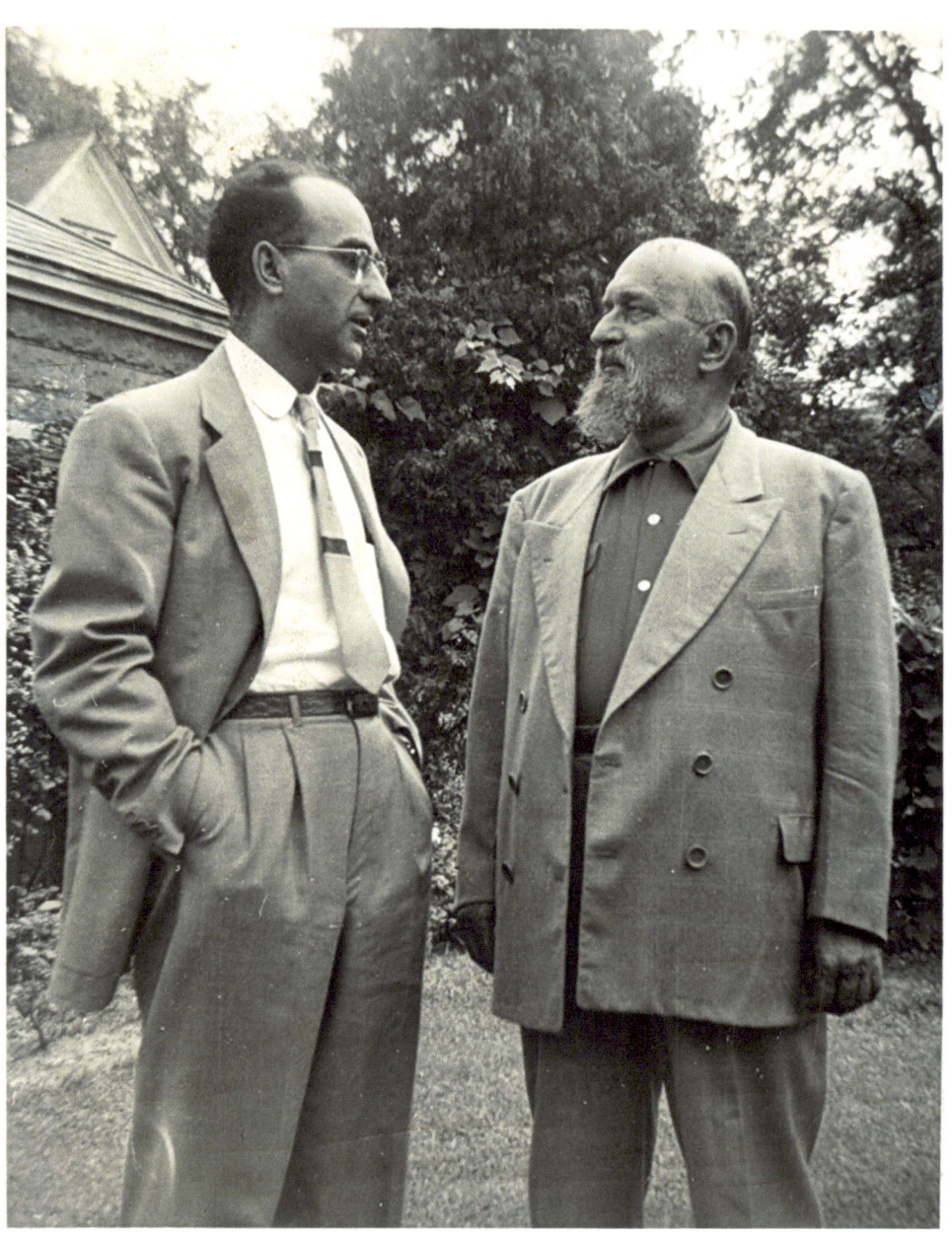

Anthony Eterovich and Ivan Meštrović 1955

Anthony William Eterovich
1916-2011 Cleveland, OH
anthonyeterovich.org

Education
1938 CIA – Full Scholarship
1941 Western Reserve University – Bachelor of Science in Education
1947 WRU - MA in Art Education
1948 – 1949 Extended Studies Ohio University
1950 – 1954 New York Art Students League

Selected Exhibitions & Awards: Solo, 2-person, group exhibitions

1934-1971 Cleveland, OH, *Cleveland Museum of Art May Shows* – 55 works, records online, May Show Database, Ingalls Library

1939-1972 Youngstown, OH, *Butler Institute of American Art* – 12 works, programs avble.

1945-1946 Eleven Colleges, Ohio Paint Makers Traveling Shows

1950 Athens, OH, *8th Annual Valley Show*, Ohio University

1951 Youngstown, OH, First Prize Purchase Award National, *16th Annual New Year's Show*, Butler Institute for American Art

1951 New York City, NY, *Downtown Gallery*, E. Halpert, Director, Special Mention NY Times

1955 Columbus, OH, 2nd Prize, *Ohio State Fair*

1956 Cleveland, OH, Women's City Club *Solo Show* 22 oil & water color paintings

1951-2003 Cleveland, OH, *Cleveland Institute of Art Faculty Shows*

1963 Cleveland, OH, InTown Club *Solo Show* Charcoal Drawings

1963 New York City, Long Island, Cleveland, *30 Cleveland Artists*, YWCA, UNAC & Circle Galleries

1964 Cleveland, OH – Jewish Community Center of Cleveland – *Artistic Excellence*

Collections
Artists Archives of the Western Reserve
ARTneo
Butler Institute of American Art
Canton Art Institute (1950-51)
Cleveland Museum of Art
Goodyear Corporation
Massillon Museum (1971)
Southern Ohio Museum

Current Honors/Exhibitions

2014 Classroom named for AE, Cleve. Inst. Of Art
2015 *Sustenance, from Palate to Palette*, AAWR
2015 *Fractured Planes*, ARTneo
2016 *A Thrilling Act*, Tregoning & Co.
2016 *Fundamental Gestures*, ARTneo
2016 *Out of the Archives*, AAWR @ BCC
2016 CIA Study Collection
2018 *Three Angles*, ARTneo& AAWR,CANTriennial
2018 *A Thrilling Act* Tour begins @ SOMACC

Professional Experience

1941 – 1978 – Cleveland, OH, Cleveland Public Schools, Art Teacher including Chair, Art Dept. James Rhodes High School, 1962-1978

1943-45 – Indian Town Gap, PA and Camp Gordon Johnston, Carabelle, FL., U.S. Army Sergeant Tech Four – portraits, maps, posters.

1951-2005 Cleveland, OH, Cleveland Institute of Art – Evening, Weekend, & Summer Instructor

1981-1989, Cleveland, OH, Chair, Regional Scholastic Art Competition

Publications, Reviews
New York Times, Cleveland Plain Dealer, Cleveland Press, Sun Post, Cleveland Scene, CAN Journal, Sound of Applause, WVIZ 1947-2016

La Revue Moderne, ©December 1, 1960

Painting the Spirit of Nature by Maxine Masterfield, ©1984

AAWR would like to thank the following supporters:

The Bernice and David E. Davis Art Foundation
The George Gund Foundation
The William Bingham Foundation
The Zufall Foundation

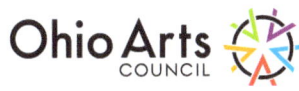

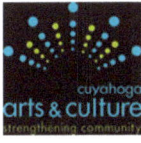 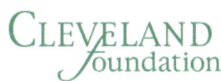

The Artists Archives of the Western Reserve (AAWR)
is a unique archival facility and regional museum created to preserve
representative bodies of work by Ohio visual artists.

Through ongoing research, exhibition, and educational programs the AAWR
actively documents and promotes this cultural heritage for the benefit of the public.

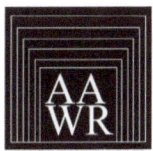

www.ingramcontent.com/pod-product-compliance
Lightning Source LLC
Chambersburg PA
CBHW040415220526
45473CB00004B/1243